in the Glass Booth

A DRAMA IN TWO ACTS

By Robert Shaw

SAMUEL FRENCH, INC.

45 West 25th Street   NEW YORK, N.Y. 10010
7623 Sunset Boulevard   HOLLYWOOD 90046
LONDON   *TORONTO*

THE MAN IN THE GLASS BOOTH, by Robert Shaw, directed by Harold Pinter, was presented at the Royale Theatre, New York.

CHARACTERS
(*In Order of Their Appearance*)

GOLDMAN	*Donald Pleasance*
SAM	*Graham Brown*
JACK	*Madison Arnold*
CHARLIE COHN	*Lawrence Pressman*
FLOWER MAN	*John Coe*
DR. KESSEL	*Jack Hollander*
RUDIN	*F. Murray Abraham*
MRS. ROSEN	*Ronni L. Gilbert*
STEIGER	*Paul Manfred*
DURER	*Michael Ebert*
PRESIDING JUDGE	*Boris Tumarin*
JUDGES	*Martin Rudy, Ben Kapin*
MRS. LEVI	*Florence Tarlow*
PROSECUTOR	*Jack Hollander*
OLD MAN MAROWSKI	*Madison Arnold*
TZELNIKER	*F. Murray Abraham*
LANDAU	*Abe Vigoda*
MRS. LEHMANN	*Tresa Hughes*
SERGEANT	*Clinton Atkinson*
GUARDS	*Walter Allen, Robert Anthony*

Production Stage Manager: *John Drew Devereaux*

The play takes place in New York and Israel in 1964–1965.

3

The Man in the Glass Booth

ACT ONE

SCENE 1

The Verdi Requiem on a fine Autumn morning.

A bald-headed MAN *in a silk dressing-gown prays beside
a tomb. A masterpiece rests upon an easel. A glass
ELEVATOR rises into one side of the room: doors
and a hall lead off; one of the doors is locked.
French windows open to a roof garden full of statues,
artificial flowers and artificial trees. Beyond the
garden rise the peaks of Manhattan. A BELL sounds
the hour; eight o'clock. Into the room come* TWO
SERVANTS *carrying a masterpiece. They change this
masterpiece for the masterpiece already on the easel.
They leave the room. The* SERVANTS *re-enter,* ONE
*with morning coffee which he sets down beside a
chair, and switches on a STOCKMASTER; the*
OTHER *with silk jacket, a tie and a bowl of water.
The* SERVANTS *wait;* GOLDMAN *rises from his knees.
He dusts the urn, and puts the duster into his dressing-gown pocket, goes to his chair. His colored valet,*
SAM, *takes his silk dressing gown, washes his* EM-
PLOYER'S *hands, while* JACK, *Goldman's butler, pours
his* EMPLOYER'S *coffee.* GOLDMAN *sits in the chair
gazing all the while at the Stockmaster.* JACK *leaves
the room.* SAM *ties his* EMPLOYER'S *tie, slips on his*
EMPLOYER'S *jacket.* CHARLIE COHN, *Goldman's sec-
retary, enters, carrying the New York dailies, which
he gives to* SAM, *who puts them on the desk.*

CHARLIE. Good morning, Mr. Goldman.

(*But there is no answer.* CHARLIE COHN *goes and seats himself on the love seat, prepares to take notes.* GOLDMAN *sips his coffee.*)

GOLDMAN. Switch off the Requiem. (SAM *switches off the REQUIEM, and then the STOCKMASTER.*) The market's very good.
SAM. Should I sell?
GOLDMAN. Hold. I'll pass you the word.

(GOLDMAN *turns and stares at the painting, presses a bell. Rises.* CHARLIE *rises.* JACK *enters.*)

JACK. Yes, Mr. Goldman?
GOLDMAN. I'm bored with the Rembrandt, bring in a Poussin.
JACK. Which one, sir?
GOLDMAN. Arcadia.

(JACK *and* SAM *take down the Rembrandt, exit. Pause.*)

CHARLIE. (*Crossing to desk.*) Happy birthday, Mr. Goldman.
GOLDMAN. How's Momma?
CHARLIE. Never better, thank you, Mr. Goldman.
GOLDMAN. That woman ought to go on a diet. Birthday? You say it's my birthday?
CHARLIE. Yes, Mr. Goldman.
GOLDMAN. (*Reading the front page.*) Friday the 20th of November 1964. How old am I, Charlie?
CHARLIE. You're fifty-two, Mr. Goldman.
GOLDMAN. Thank you, Charlie. (SAM *re-enters.*) What's the temperature outside?
SAM. Fahrenheit or Centigrade?
GOLDMAN. You know my preference.
SAM. Forty-one and a half.

GOLDMAN. Go down to the cuisine and sample the cheesecake.

SAM. Yes, sir! (SAM *goes out, taking the valet stand.*)

GOLDMAN. (*Crossing below desk to* U. L. C.) Forty-one and a half. (*Pause.*) If I wasn't so old I'd don my vicuna. Matilda always adored me in my vicuna. (*Pause.*) It's a house without a woman, Charlie. (*Pause.*) I ought to get a new wife.

CHARLIE. Yes, Mr. Goldman.

GOLDMAN. (*Sits on the love seat.*) I should bring in naked servants. Naked black female servants.

CHARLIE. That would be very delightful, Mr. Goldman.

GOLDMAN. Miss America. Miss America 1964. That's what I need. I'd knock her up in no time. (*Waving his hand.*) It's all these empty closets that's gettin' me down. All these coathangers with no frocks on 'em. A man without a woman . . . a man without a woman . . . (GOLDMAN *sighs.*) Maybe I got to go for intelligence . . . maybe I need one of those reporters . . . one of those Time and Life—long-legged—Washington—Posts . . . one of those articulates. (GOLDMAN *sighs again. Rises, crosses to desk and sits.*) When are we due at the Banks?

CHARLIE. Eleven-o-five at the Irving Trust. Eleven-twenty-two the Bank of Montreal. Eleven-forty-seven the Trade and twelve-thirty-five the Chase Manhattan.

GOLDMAN. When do I see Levinsky?

CHARLIE. He's coming from Boston this afternoon, Mr. Goldman.

GOLDMAN. Call Schwab—tell him I'm in.

CHARLIE. For how much, Mr. Goldman?

GOLDMAN. All the way, all the way. He's my blood brother, Charlie. Charlie, the thing about a wife is . . . Where do I go tonight?

CHARLIE. (*Sits on love seat.*) The opera tonight, Mr. Goldman. You're escorting the Duchess. And there's twenty-two begging letters this morning.

GOLDMAN. Give 'em all somethin' but not too much. (*Pause.*) Listen, when you call Schwab tell him my limit's a hundred thousand: I think you're right there, I think you made a substantial point. Hey, I don't like that Bernstein, do you?

CHARLIE. No I don't, Mr. Goldman.

GOLDMAN. No. No, I don't like that Bernstein.

CHARLIE. I don't trust him, Mr. Goldman.

GOLDMAN. I don't trust him neither, Charlie. (*Pause.*) Charlie, maybe I ought to go for one of those news announcers—maybe I ought to get me one of these weather-girls. Hey, call O'Brien—white-curtained walls for Lexington.

CHARLIE. Top to bottom?

GOLDMAN. All but the penthouses. Up there we'll have gold. Gotta give the parrots somethin' to live in—you follow?

CHARLIE. Yes, I follow.

GOLDMAN. Who's comin' to the game tomorrow?

CHARLIE. Mr. Winkler, Mr. Hochschild, the Senators and the Mayor.

GOLDMAN. (*Upset.*) No ladies!

CHARLIE. No, sir. Not as yet.

GOLDMAN. Charlie! Charlie! Invite somebody beautiful, will ya? I can't spend the entire afternoon with those bums. Imagine the drive back, Charlie.

CHARLIE. If I may say so it will be cold out there in the Stadium, Mr. Goldman—the forecast . . .

GOLDMAN. So get me some sables with interior electric currents—build in some cabinets of champagne and put a few scent sprays in the collars. I gotta have somebody pretty to look at, Charlie! And nothin' common! I gotta have somebody with a face. Somebody with bones. Somebody aristocratic, Charlie! See if Garbo's in town.

CHARLIE. (*Rises and crosses L. of* GOLDMAN.) Yes, Mr. Goldman. Mr. Goldman, on Sunday your guests will be picked up by the autobus in geographical order—I have worked that out very carefully—they will arrive at the lake-side in Westchester at approximately ten-twenty-seven—I have synchronized the fireworks personally and will set off the first rocket as the autobus descends the hill.

GOLDMAN. Thank you, Charlie. (*He smiles.*) They'll like my bus.

CHARLIE. I think they will, Mr. Goldman.

GOLDMAN. I don't suppose none of 'em's bin in a bus for twenty years.

CHARLIE. Perhaps longer, Mr. Goldman. Perhaps never.

GOLDMAN. Is there a bed in there for Mrs. Weissbart?

CHARLIE. Of course, Mr. Goldman. Up beside the driver.

GOLDMAN. Good. Yeah, well they'll all like my bus. The first bus I ever remember had a clock in it. I went to Tannhauser and the bus had a clock. My mother used to sing like Flagstad. Listen, when I'm at the architect's get down to Parke Bernet. Make me a bid for that Tigerware jug.

CHARLIE. The one with the silver mount.

GOLDMAN. The 1560.

CHARLIE. What shall I go to?

GOLDMAN. Just get it. (*He looks at his watch.*) How long do we have now?

CHARLIE. Forty-two minutes.

GOLDMAN. All right. All right, dear Charlie, while I'm ponderin' on Madison read me some more of this brochure you're writing for us. (GOLDMAN *picks up a newspaper.*)

CHARLIE. (*Taking his brochure out of the folder and sits on love seat.*) "It was in the golden spring of 1947, at about the time the Pelican building project was about to rise—"

GOLDMAN. (*Not looking up from the paper.*) Cut out that "golden." And "ascend"—"about to ascend." I'm not too old for the ladies, Charlie—don't think that. No, I'm not too old for the Princesses. It's just that I gotta have class.

CHARLIE. "Was about to ascend into the blue skies—"

GOLDMAN. Cut out that "blue."

CHARLIE. "Was about to ascend into the skies that the

beginnings of the lease to the MacTavish Publishing Company were planted—"

GOLDMAN. That the seeds of the lease were "sown," Charlie. Seeds and sown. If you have a seed you sow it . . . you follow?

CHARLIE. Yes.

GOLDMAN. Babies. Maybe I gotta have babies.

CHARLIE. "In 1947 Mr. Arthur Goldman, who was then only a junior broker—"

GOLDMAN. Maybe I ought to have a fertility test.

CHARLIE. "—was negotiating a sub-lease with the Mac-Tavish Organization on Fifth Avenue—"

GOLDMAN. Billy Goldstein's dead!

CHARLIE. Oh, dear—

GOLDMAN. Very orthodox. Very donating, that Billy. Jesus! The Pope's forgiven the Jews. Jesus. The Pope has forgiven the Jews.

CHARLIE. "—because the MacTavish Organization wanted to move to Park Avenue. It was at this point that Mr. Arthur Goldman had the first of his many brilliant ideas. While canvassing Manhattan for potential customers for the building about to be vacated by MacTavish, he happened to get into the elevator with the young lady who worked at the MacTavish reception desk. 'Good morning, Mr.—' " (*Looks at* GOLDMAN *and rises.*) Excuse me, are you feeling faint?

GOLDMAN. Continue.

CHARLIE. " 'Good morning, Mr. Goldman,' she said, 'and how is everything with you this fine morning?' "

GOLDMAN. What a horrible voice you got, Charlie.

CHARLIE. I'm sorry, Mr. Goldman.

GOLDMAN. Let's have quiet till we get to the Banks. (*Pause.*) So the Pope has forgiven the Jews. And to think poor Billy Goldstein didn't live to know it. (JACK *and* SAM *enter with the Arcadia.* GOLDMAN *and* COHN *watch in silence as they hang it up.* GOLDMAN *goes to Arcadia, places a hand on* JACK'S *shoulder, looks at it.*) This guy Poussin needed beauty—he wanted to return to innocence.

Calm and sunny, beautiful young men . . . dignified young women . . . shepherds . . . death reigns . . . but has not terror. Even in Arcady death is. You follow? Do you think they'll cable poor Billy Goldstein in Arcady, Jack?

JACK. Was he a painter too, Mr. Goldman?

GOLDMAN. (*Grinning.*) Take it out and leave an empty space, in memory of poor Billy Goldstein. (JACK *and* SAM *go, taking Arcadia with them.*) Get the Pope on the television.

CHARLIE. What?

GOLDMAN. We have thirteen channels—he has to be on one of 'em. (CHARLIE COHN *goes to the TELEVISION, turns it on. The HOUSE-PHONE rings;* COHN *answers it.*) Nobody in here but us Jews.

CHARLIE. Yes . . . ? The fresh flowers, Mr. Goldman.

GOLDMAN. Okay, okay. So get me the Pope.

CHARLIE. Elevator's coming down. (CHARLIE *hangs up the house-phone, goes to the television.*) Many Happy Returns, Mr. Goldman.

GOLDMAN. Thank you, thank you. Try the educational. Try thirteen. When was the Pope made infallible? Don't answer that question. (*The ELEVATOR leaves the room and slides down.*) So the Pope has absolved the Jews, eh?

CHARLIE. Yes.

GOLDMAN. And I always thought it was J.C. himself who did that . . . Jesus, there he is! We got him in color.

(GOLDMAN *runs to the television beside* CHARLIE COHN. *They watch the broadcast from Rome.*)

COMMENTATOR. And now the Pope takes his seat between his two senior Cardinal deacons, Alfredo Cardinal Ottaviani, seventy-four years old, and Alberto Cardinal de Jorio, eighty years old. The Pope is dressed in his—

GOLDMAN. Turn down the sound. I make my own comments from now on. Let's cut out all this schtick. (*As

CHARLIE COHN *turns down the SOUND so that it becomes indistinguishable, the ELEVATOR slides into the room again and a* MAN *of Goldman's own weight and age, dressed in a smart suit, loaded with artificial flower plants, steps out of it.* CHARLIE *hurries to help and to lead him to the roof-garden but* GOLDMAN *does not turn round and sits absorbed, making his comments.*) Hey, he's giving the Virgin Mary a new title—I can see that. Monsignor Dante's fumbling for his handkerchief— Monsignor Dante's bustin' into tears . . . The Arabs must be . . . bustin' into tears . . . The Fuehrer said: "Es darf Nunmehr fur die welt hein Fuehrer oder ein mann, jetz spricht das deutsche Volk . . ." The Fuehrer said . . . "No longer speaks one man but the German people . . ." The Fuehrer said, "Your Holiness: In order to carry on his existence as a parasite on other peoples, the Judlein is forced to deny his inner nature. The more intelligent the individual Jew is, the more . . . the more he will succeed in this deception." (*Turning around to* CHARLIE.) God bless America, we got him in color, Charlie. (*As* GOLDMAN *turns he sees* CHARLIE *and the* MAN *who brought the flowers in coming back from the roof-garden, and something about this* FLOWER MAN *startles* GOLDMAN.) Hey. . . . I know you.

FLOWER MAN. Sir?

GOLDMAN. I know you. (*Pause.*) You know I know you.

FLOWER MAN. I've delivered here before.

(*Pause.*)

GOLDMAN. My mistake, then.

CHARLIE. All right, Mr. Goldman?

GOLDMAN. My mistake. (CHARLIE COHN *nods to the* FLOWER MAN, *who leaves.*) I'm sorry, Mr. Cohn. A likeness.

CHARLIE. Sir?

GOLDMAN. Lace my coffee. (*As* COHN *pours brandy into Goldman's coffee,* GOLDMAN *sits down, staring ahead, frowning. Rising.*) A moment of privacy, please.

(COHN *leaves the room.* GOLDMAN *swallows coffee and brandy. A long silence, then the ELEVATOR re-enters the room, the* FLOWER MAN *gets out again.*)

FLOWER MAN. I left my hat.

GOLDMAN. Your hat?

FLOWER MAN. Yes. (*The* FLOWER MAN *crosses Up-stage a step and turns back.*)

GOLDMAN. You've lost weight.

FLOWER MAN. Sir? (*The* FLOWER MAN *smiles.*)

GOLDMAN. Every time I say somethin' to you, you smile at me. (*The* FLOWER MAN *smiles again.*) Where's your hat?

FLOWER MAN. I must have left it someplace else. (*The* FLOWER MAN *enters the ELEVATOR and disappears.*)

(GOLDMAN *stares blankly about him, goes to the tele-vision set.* GOLDMAN *switches off the TELEVISION, shouts:*)

GOLDMAN. Charlie. (*When* CHARLIE COHN *enters, run-ning to* R. *of desk.*) Check up on that guy.

CHARLIE. The Flower Man?

GOLDMAN. (*Crossing below desk to above love seat.*) Put Arnold onto it . . . have him followed. I'm not going to the Banks. I'm not goin' to the office on this day . . . And you stay here.

CHARLIE. Sir?

GOLDMAN. Tell Momma you're sleepin' here from now on. (*Pause.*) I need you, Jewish Charlie. (*Pause.*) It's all this wealth . . . it goes to one's . . . (*Pause.*) Was he wearin' a hat? When he came in here, was he wearin' a hat?

CHARLIE. I don't think so, Mr. Goldman.

(*Pause.*)

GOLDMAN. You see, Charlie, the thing about my American wife, Matilda, was . . . she restored me. (*The ELE-VATOR ascends.*) Who's this? My cousin again?

CHARLIE. (*Looking at his watch.*) It'll be Doctor Kessel, Mr. Goldman.

(*But* GOLDMAN *has crossed abruptly to the locked door. He opens the various locks and enters. The ELE-VATOR doors open and* DR. KESSEL *gets out.*)

KESSEL. Morning, Charlie.
CHARLIE. Morning, Dr. Kessel.

(GOLDMAN *comes out of the locked room carrying a gun.*)

KESSEL. (*Puts his bag on the desk.*) Morning, Mr. Goldman. What's the matter, Mr. Goldman?
GOLDMAN. Anybody who needs vitamins has got something wrong with them. Give 'em to Charlie. (*Pause.* DR. KESSEL *laughs.*) Take your syringe and stick it up Charlie. (*Pause.* GOLDMAN *waves his gun.*) I kid you not.
CHARLIE. I don't mind, Doctor Kessel.
KESSEL. It's only B-12.

(CHARLIE COHN *takes off his jacket, takes down his trousers.* DR. KESSEL *gives him the injection. A pause. Then* GOLDMAN *laughs and laughs.* GOLDMAN *puts his gun away.*)

GOLDMAN. Sorry to bother you, fellas. Just a psychiatrist re-proving a point to his friends. Sit down, Doc. One moment, I'll pour you a drink. You took me back a bit right there. (*He brings trolley Downstage to* R. *of desk.*)
KESSEL. It's a little early for me to drink, Mr. Goldman. (*Sits desk chair.*)
GOLDMAN. I'll pay for your time. Put it on the bill. Jack! Charlie, weren't you going to your tailor—today—your tailor one of ours? (*He closes the vault.*)
CHARLIE. Yes, Mr. Goldman.

GOLDMAN. Call him up—tell him we're having a party. Tell him we'll have your fitting up here. Tell him I'll pay him for his time. You know that flower guy's name, Charlie?

CHARLIE. No, Mr. Goldman.

GOLDMAN. That flower guy's name was Dorff. D.O.-R.F.F. Dorff. Cousin Adolf, Charlie. Cousin Adolf Dorff.

(CHARLIE *goes to the phone.* JACK *enters.*)

JACK. Yes, Mr. Goldman?

GOLDMAN. Bourbon, and beers for chasers. (JACK *goes to the trolley and starts to pour.* CHARLIE *begins to talk to his tailor on the phone.*) You see, Doc, I can't go out. I'm under observation. They're on to me. I've got to stay here with you guys and work somethin' out. Don't think I'm fevered. As I recall, the Fuehrer said— (*To* JACK.) Get lost, Jack. (GOLDMAN *takes the bourbon from* JACK, *and* JACK *goes out.*) The Fuehrer said: "In the Jewish people the will to self-sacrifice does not go beyond the individual's naked instinct for self-preservation." Not a bad writer. (GOLDMAN *hands out the drinks.*) The Fuehrer said: "Is there any form of filth, any form of profligacy, particularly in cultural life, without at least one Jew involved in it? Cut even cautiously into such an abscess, you find like a maggot in a rotting body, often, dazzled by the sudden light—ein Judlein." Those vitamins got to you yet?

CHARLIE. Not yet.

GOLDMAN. Not feelin' sexy?

CHARLIE. No, Mr. Goldman.

GOLDMAN. It's slow then, slow . . . I known 'em take quicker than this. (GOLDMAN *takes a comb out of* CHARLIE'S *pocket, holds it under his nose as a moustache, throws out his arm in a Hitler salute and shouts, high-pitched.*) Remember me!

KESSEL. Yes, I—I remember all that, Mr. Goldman—

(*But abruptly* GOLDMAN *downs his drink, and goes into*

the locked room. KESSEL *looks at* CHARLIE COHN, COHN *gives* KESSEL *a bewildered shrug.*)

CHARLIE. He's never not gone to the banks.

KESSEL. What's he doing with that gun?

CHARLIE. (*Pointing at the locked door.*) Out of there. I never knew he had one.

KESSEL. What else is in there?

CHARLIE. I don't know. (JACK *enters with a tray of beer, which he takes to the trolley.* CHARLIE *stops talking, looks at* JACK, *who is opening the beer, and then continues speaking.*) I've never been in there. None of us has ever been in there. (*Pause.*) Valuables, I suppose. (*Pause.*) Maybe some things of his late wife, Matilda's. I don't know, I've never been in there. (JACK *exits.*)

KESSEL. Who cleans it?

CHARLIE. He cleans it.

KESSEL. Who's this cousin Dorff?

CHARLIE. I am bewildered, Doctor Kessel.

(*But* GOLDMAN *comes back.*)

GOLDMAN. One quarter of the city's Jewish . . . I've been considering my buildings, my palaces . . . I've been givin' my work a moment's thought. When's your tailor comin' up?

CHARLIE. Right away, Mr. Goldman.

GOLDMAN. Have him checked at the door. Is he a blue-blooded American three-generation Hebrew?

CHARLIE. Oh, yes, Mr. Goldman.

GOLDMAN. Know his voice?

CHARLIE. Anywhere.

GOLDMAN. Check it on the phone. Have him speak to you. I want no more Flower Guys up here. Not with no wreaths. (GOLDMAN *refills all glasses.*) Perhaps I'm missing my Matilda today, Doc. A good clean-livin' all embracin'— (*Originally* Swedish.) American gal. Naive enough to restore me. Didn't know too much . . . you follow? But sexy. Very lovin'. Very passionate. Very sensual-spiritual. Made a great noise. That's why I polish her urn, Doc. (GOLDMAN *drinks deep*.) Which one of my palaces do you prefer, Doc? Which one of my temples most takes your eye?

KESSEL. I like very much that new apartment house on Lexington and Fifty-seventh.

GOLDMAN. You don't hear none of your neighbors' love life in those bathrooms. Yes, I remember them all, Doc. I shared Scott Fitzgerald's bed, sat naked with him in the Astor Bar—that's why I made no bid for the Astor—

KESSEL. When are you taking your vacation, Mr. Goldman?

GOLDMAN. Charlie, did you know Scotty and I swam in Zelda's panties, in the Pulitzer Fountain before the Plaza Hotel? I had the pink, he had the purple.

CHARLIE. I didn't know that, sir! No, I didn't know you knew the Fitzgeralds.

GOLDMAN. Oh, yes indeedy. We drove on the roofs of our landaus from Broadway to Washington Square. Call me a liar, Charlie. Up through Harlem where they all threw tickertape—the only good Hebrew's a black one—we finished at Childs for breakfast. After the cheesecake, I said to Scotty: "Let's go to the morgue," and by God, he and Papa rattles us all downtown and we had a cup of coffee with the stiffs.

KESSEL. I think you *are* a little bit fevered, Mr. Goldman.

GOLDMAN. Don't you call me a liar.

KESSEL. I wouldn't dream of it.

GOLDMAN. Don't you call me a liar. Let's sit quiet. Let's pay our respects. (GOLDMAN *sits on the love seat;* CHARLIE D. L. *Long pause*.) Doc, I'm seeking both to inspire and distract myself.

KESSEL. From what?

GOLDMAN. From the arbeit-macht-frei grey stone edifices . . . the innumerable three-floor-high-identical-edifices. Charlie, you call this a metropolis . . . that place

. . . that place . . . was boundless. Being an athlete stood me in good stead. Sing me the Internationale, Charlie, move me, render me, rape my senses. From the dead, Doc, from the dead. It's my birthday, you see.

KESSEL. Oh. Many happy returns.

CHARLIE. I'm sorry I don't know that song, Mr. Goldman.

GOLDMAN. Then you're in neglect. It's the living who are in neglect. It's not ended, you know. (*Rises, crosses* c.) What can we do for the living? (*Very quietly*.) The last time I saw Dorff . . . the last time but one I saw my cousin Dorff, he was goin' from bed to bed, from litter to litter, from place to place . . . with his pistol. He was tappin' them on their domes with the barrel, he was testin' their brains out, he was listenin' to see what was hollow. One, two, three, not another sound but the echo. Bang, bang, bang and I bring up the trolley. (*The PHONE rings.* CHARLIE *goes to the phone, picks it up*.) Check the voice!

CHARLIE. Hello. What? No. No. You must have the wrong number. This is Mr. Arthur Goldman's residence.

GOLDMAN. (*Exploding, snatches away the phone and hangs up*.) What you tell him that for? Idiot. You don't tell nobody nothin' from now on.

CHARLIE. I'm sorry.

GOLDMAN. A foreign voice?

CHARLIE. No, an American voice.

GOLDMAN. (*Crosses to the trolley*.) That wasn't no wrong number. And that was a foreign voice. (*Pause*.) The *first* time I saw that Dorff was early . . . wanted to knock up my sister. He was thirteen years old at the time . . . I do believe he made it. (*Silence. Then HOUSE-PHONE rings.* CHARLIE COHN *looks at his* EMPLOYER.) Pick it up.

CHARLIE. It's Mr. Rudin, Mr. Goldman.

GOLDMAN. Rudin?

CHARLIE. My tailor, Mr. Goldman.

GOLDMAN. Is he Kosher?

CHARLIE. One hundred percent, Mr. Goldman.

GOLDMAN. Nobody's one hundred percent. Ask him if he's got tape with him.

CHARLIE. Have you got your tape with you? Oh, yes, Mr. Goldman.

GOLDMAN. Have him come up.

CHARLIE. Mr. Goldman says to come up.

(CHARLIE *puts down the phone. Pause. The ELEVATOR descends.* GOLDMAN *pours another Bourbon into a fresh glass.* GOLDMAN *laughs. Pause.* GOLDMAN *becomes absorbed. The elevator ascends,* GOLDMAN *takes out his pistol.*)

GOLDMAN. In Israel they can't even define it. J . . . E . . . W. Can't define that word in Israel. They got Councils workin' at it: Boards and Councils. (*To* CHARLIE.) Identify him. We're all Germans, Charlie. All Germans and all J . . . E . . . W's. So identify him.

(CHARLIE *runs to the ELEVATOR; as soon as it arrives, he calls hurriedly.*)

CHARLIE. It's Rudin, Mr. Goldman.

(*Putting away the gun, beaming,* GOLDMAN *advances toward the elevator with outstretched hand.*)

GOLDMAN. What do you think of the Pope's edict, Rudin?

RUDIN. Who needs it?

GOLDMAN. Spoken like a Democrat. Charlie, put on Deany. C 12, B 13. Have you got a quarter?

CHARLIE. Yes. sir. Right here. (CHARLIE COHN *goes to the JUKE BOX, puts in a quarter, and presses the buttons.*)

GOLDMAN. Do you go to the ball games, Rudin?

RUDIN. Yes, sir.

GOLDMAN. See the last of Y. A. Tittle?

RUDIN. Yes, sir, I did.

GOLDMAN. (*Gives* RUDIN *a drink and takes the suit.*) Catch up, we're ahead of you. Jack! Seat yourself. What are you wearing under the vicuna? Silk?

RUDIN. No, sir, mohair.

(JACK *enters. A Dean Martin RECORD comes on.*)

GOLDMAN. Take the Levite tailor's vicuna. (GOLDMAN *holds up his hand, dances a while with the suit, takes* RUDIN'S *coat and gives them to* JACK, *who exits. Smiling at* RUDIN.) Can't wear a vicuna when you're old. Rudin, I discovered the secret of America twenty-five years ago . . . a silk suit and a vicuna . . . what a young man needs to make it. In the winter you wear the coat . . . when you get into the steam-heat you take the coat off . . . in the summer you carry the vicuna over your arm and when you get into the air-conditioning you put the vicuna on . . . only way to stay alive in America . . . the thing was, Rudin Yiddle, Doc Yiddle, Charlie Yiddle, a large part died because of the hazards of the weather . . . Take the measurements, Rudin.

RUDIN. I already have Mr. Cohn's measurements, Mr. Goldman.

GOLDMAN. Not Charlie's. Mine.

KESSEL. Might I replenish my glass? (KESSEL *does so and sits* D. R.)

(RUDIN *begins to measure* GOLDMAN *and writes the figures in a small notebook.*)

GOLDMAN. On this day we get loaded. This is the day I was . . . chosen . . . you follow? This is the day I was born. Correct me if I'm wrong, Rudin. Charlie, gently. I gotta protect myself. (CHARLIE COHN *adjusts the CONTROLS. Dean Martin sings gently.*) Correct me if I'm wrong, Rudin. When Y. A. Tittle comes back the New

York Giants are down. He hits Joe Morrison on the Browns' forty-nine. He calls Gifford on a square-out to the sidelines in front of Parrish. He gets the ball on a two count. He goes straight back. He's covered by three, he holds up the ball, he throws to the sideline as Gifford fakes . . . all of his life was in that pass . . . that I know, boys. Y.A.'s last game . . . you follow? The ball was almost in Gifford's hands when Bernie Parrish picked it out of the air, and Bernie Parrish ran straight down the line. So Y.A. lost the ball on a square-out. He's been playing square-outs for thirty years. Fifty-two-twenty the final. At the end Gary Wood is running the team, and he, Y. A. Tittle, is benched. Okay, Rudin?

RUDIN. Right.

GOLDMAN. Don't forget the head.

RUDIN. What?

(GOLDMAN *points to his head. Another Dean Martin RECORD comes on, softly.*)

GOLDMAN. Y.A. said he wished he could have given the people a little more to finish up with. Gentlemen, my will is in my treasure house. A Hebrew, your highnesses, can't get converted because how can he bring himself to believe in the divinity of another Hebrew . . . German fellow-citizens, I . . . in German law . . . there is a time limit . . . as a zoologist, there are no villains . . . no villains and no heroes . . . Gentlemen, once I was passionate. I WAS PASSIONATE. (*Abruptly,* GOLDMAN *screams in anguish:* DR. KESSEL *rises,* CHARLIE *rises,* RUDIN *rises.*) Sit down. (RUDIN *sits on the love seat.*) Be seated, Doc, I don't need you. (KESSEL *sits.*) Just an old wound opening up . . . I'll close it. I'll close it when I work it out . . . you follow? (SAM *and* JACK *come running in to* C. GOLDMAN *crosses up.*) You guys kosher?

SAM. No, sir.

GOLDMAN. (*Affectionately.*) Get lost, then. Take the day. TAKE THE DAY OFF. Go to the race-track, fellas.

Here. (GOLDMAN *throws them a roll of banknotes.*) Get in the elevator and have the day on me. (SAM *and* JACK *get into the ELEVATOR and descend.* GOLDMAN *takes notebook from* RUDIN *and sits at the desk.*) What size shoes do I take, Charlie?

CHARLIE. Seven and a half.

GOLDMAN. Read to me, Charlie? Give me time to reflect. I got the image. It's the details that bother me.

(CHARLIE COHN *switches off the JUKEBOX.* GOLDMAN *smiles.* CHARLIE COHN *comes back to his brochure, reads.*)

CHARLIE. (L. *of desk.*) "Mr. Arthur Goldman's latest building is a thirty-two million dollar transaction. It is called the 'Friday Evening Building' as a result of a lease for about one quarter of the building's total space to Mac-Tavish Publishing Company, publishers of the world-famous 'Friday Evening Playgirl' and several other leading—"

GOLDMAN. Rudin, make Charlie a couple of cashmeres and a vicuna. Since I'm old, make me a saxony, and a blue gaberdine with a removable fur. How are your patients taking it, Doc?

KESSEL. Taking what?

GOLDMAN. How are *your* clients gonna take it, Rudin?

RUDIN. Some of my customers are over-eager for acceptance, Mr. Goldman.

GOLDMAN. (*Pleased.*) You're smart, Rudin . . . you follow my drift. The Pope's edict, Doc. Religion. Religion's the stabilizing force, Rudin. If you can't get in through the clubs, you gotta get in through the charities. You're smart, Rudin. D'you carry a gun?

RUDIN. No.

GOLDMAN. I'm looking for a bodyguard. No special Jewish guilt in the Crucifixion, eh? Rudin, do you spit on that?

RUDIN. Yes, I do.

GOLDMAN. Doc, do you spit on that?

KESSEL. No, I don't, Mr. Goldman, I think—

GOLDMAN. (*Coldly.*) Doc, I spit on all these Cardinals and all these Rabbis. (*Pause.*) Where you goin' for your vacation, Rudin? Palm Beach? Know any good Krauts, Rudin?

RUDIN. Miami.

GOLDMAN. Take your golf clubs?

RUDIN. Yes, sir.

GOLDMAN. Great. You'll do well. Charlie. Charlie, do you spit on all these Cardinals and all these Rabbis?

CHARLIE. Oh, yes, Mr. Goldman; yes, I spit on all these Cardinals and Rabbis.

(*Long pause.*)

GOLDMAN. Thank you, Charlie. (*Pause.* GOLDMAN *rises, draws his pistol, whistling "Rosamunda."*) On your feet, scum. (*The* TWO MEN *jump up.*) This isn't a rest cure. Back to work, scum. Nobody gets out except through the chimney. If you don't like it, try the electric wire. (GOLDMAN *laughs.*) Sorry to bother you, fellas. I've gotta get rid of you—I'm almost there . . . it's a matter of cunning from here on in.

KESSEL. Mr. Goldman . . . I want to give you a prescription . . .

GOLDMAN. (*Pressing the button for the elevator.*) Never argue with a drunk, Doc—haven't been saner in my life. You come around tomorrow. Charlie, get Mr. Rudin's vicuna. Back to your rags, Rudin. Got my measurements?

RUDIN. Yes, sir.

GOLDMAN. (*Laughing.*) Let me have them. (RUDIN *does so.*) I need them for my diet. Two saxonies, a vicuna and a coffin. Doc, look in tomorrow. Drop in before Miami, Rudin. (KESSEL *and* RUDIN *go down in ELEVATOR.* CHARLIE *puts the glasses, cup and saucer on the drink trolley and wheels it Upstage into position.*) What do I pay you?

CHARLIE. Four hundred, Mr. Goldman.

GOLDMAN. Four hundred! Four hundred dollars a week!

CHARLIE. Yes, Mr. Goldman.

GOLDMAN. (*Whistling.*) I'm generous, ain't I, Charlie?

CHARLIE. You certainly are, Mr. Goldman.

(*Pause.* GOLDMAN *stares at* CHARLIE, *then smiles happily.*)

GOLDMAN. You see, Charlie . . . it don't really matter whether that Flower Guy was my cousin Dorff or not. (GOLDMAN *takes off his jacket.*) Shut the louvers.

CHARLIE. (*He does so.*) Shall I put on a light?

GOLDMAN. Yes, a soft light. (CHARLIE *does so.*) Did you buy me a birthday present? (*Crossing to* CHARLIE *above desk.*)

CHARLIE. Yes, Mr. Goldman.

GOLDMAN. You did?

CHARLIE. Of course, Mr. Goldman. Shall I get it?

GOLDMAN. No. Later. Later. Thank you, Charlie. Thank you. Go to the study, get a new line on that phone, a new number. Keep it to yourself and when you've got it— call me overseas. Let's have a breeze. Put on the fan. (CHARLIE *does as asked.*) Not freezin', young Charlie. None of your high winds of Asia blowin' over the face of the earth—no whip to it, you see. I was great at tennis, Charlie. Could have been a pro. (GOLDMAN *takes off his waistcoat and tie.*)

CHARLIE. Yes?

GOLDMAN. Keep loyal to me and I change my will. You follow?

CHARLIE. Yes, Mr. Goldman.

GOLDMAN. (*Gently placing his hand on* CHARLIE'S *shoulder.*) A man who has no shoes is a fool. I won't involve you . . . I need you, Charlie. Bear with me, and I'll not put you down. Okay? I'll be wantin' The Vatican, Cairo and Jerusalem. Okay, dear Charlie. (CHARLIE *leaves the room.* GOLDMAN *calls after him.*) Nothin' for half of

an hour. (GOLDMAN *takes off his shirt, lights a cigar from a table lighter, sings softly:*)
What bells will ring for those who died like sheep?
Dies irae, dies illa
Solvet saeclum in favilla,
What bells will ring for those who died defiled?
For those who died in excrement?
Rest eternal grant them
Light eternal shine upon them.

(GOLDMAN *holds up the cigar, draws deep on it, and holds the lighted end of the cigar under his left armpit.*)

THE CURTAIN FALLS

ACT ONE

SCENE 2

During the blackout the TAPE RECORDER begins. When the lights go on, CHARLIE COHN is sitting at GOLDMAN's desk smoking a cigar, drinking brandy, and black coffee, wearing a dressing gown.

TAPE RECORDER. (GOLDMAN's *voice.*) I don't want none of these superlatives, Charlie. You must model your style upon the masters—not upon the also-ran. On seven and ten you got too many adjectives. Remember Lexington. Remember the apartments. Artificial sunlight where they wait for their taxis and the sidewalk heated all around the block. If you want to keep Jewish, stay out of Israel. (*Pause.*) You need any cash—call Morty. Anybody asks for me, I'm spending a long Thanksgiving with a sick aunt.

(*The PHONE rings.* CHARLIE *switches off the TAPE RECORDER, picks it up.*)

CHARLIE. Hello. Oh, hello, Momma. No, you didn't wake me. I was working. Momma, as soon as he gets back I'll come right home. Tomorrow night at the earliest. Buenos Aires. Momma, I don't ask him things like that. Momma, he has sent all the servants to the country and I have strict instructions not to leave the apartment. I miss you too, Momma. I know you can't sleep without me, Momma, but you must try. Now go to sleep. Momma, you must go to sleep. Momma, take a couple of pills and go to sleep. Good night, Momma.

(CHARLIE *puts down the phone, switches on the TAPE RECORDER again.*)

TAPE RECORDER. (GOLDMAN's *voice.*) I remember them inert, Charlie. Phantoms. Crawling for bread. These people now in Manhattan, they only speak to you in a blizzard. Can't wait to check a coat. (*Pause.*) Anybody asks for me tell 'em I'm after a pedigree. Tell 'em I'm meetin' a man about a dog. Last known in Chile—present where-abouts, Brazil. (CHARLIE *stops TAPE, re-plays.*) Any-body asks for me tell 'em I'm after a pedigree. Tell 'em I'm meetin' a man about a dog. Last known in Chile—present whereabouts, Brazil. (*Pause.*) Send the servants to the country, Charlie. Give 'em some air. Keep the rooms dusted and don't forget the urn. Don't forget Matilda. If I don't reappear you can open the will. (CHARLIE *crosses to the locked door, consults a notebook, begins to open the combination lock.*) Yes, I think you'll be pleased with my testament, Charlie. And I think you'll be pleased with my palaces. Take care of my palaces, Charlie. Some of my best friends are Jews. (*Pause.*) Page seventeen—I don't like that comma. Page twenty-two, cut out the colons. Put on the Fuehrer. Charlie. Put on the Fuehrer. It might give me inspiration.

(CHARLIE *exits into the room. Then, on the TAPE RECORDER, sounds of one of Hitler's speeches. The*

ELEVATOR LIGHT comes on. The ELEVATOR door opens and GOLDMAN *enters. He stops, listens to the tape for a moment, then crosses the Stage to the desk. He quietly puts down his briefcase, turns up the VOLUME of the Hitler tape recording.* CHARLIE *comes to the door. Long pause.* GOLDMAN *turns off the TAPE.)*

CHARLIE. I didn't know you were back. I just didn't know you were back. (*Pause.*) You told me to look after everything. I was checking all the doors. I was just going to work on the brochure. I had no idea you'd returned. You said tomorrow night. Will it . . . will it change everything?

GOLDMAN. (*Points his pistol at* CHARLIE.) Charlie, you're drinkin' too much.

CHARLIE. I'm sorry, Mr. Goldman.

GOLDMAN. From now on you will address me as Colonel.

CHARLIE. I'm sorry, Colonel.

GOLDMAN. Okay. Okay. Light the fish. (CHARLIE *switches on the LIGHTS on the fish tanks.*) And feed 'em. (CHARLIE *does so.* GOLDMAN *closes the vault.*) Have you ever been in there before?

CHARLIE. Oh, no. No, I can assure you. I'm so sorry, Mr. Goldman. You see, I didn't know you were back.

GOLDMAN. Relax. The Fuehrer was always forgiving to his friends. Sit down. (GOLDMAN *smiles reassuringly.* CHARLIE *sits on love seat.*) Snow on the way?

CHARLIE. That's the forecast, Mr. Goldman.

GOLDMAN. (*Sits at the desk.*) Colonel! What Saint's being honored this December night?

CHARLIE. Shall I look it up, Colonel?

GOLDMAN. Later. Later.

(*Silence.*)

CHARLIE. Did you have a successful trip to South America, Colonel?

GOLDMAN. Since Christ appointed Saint Peter there've been two hundred and sixty-two Popes. Seventy-seven have been declared Saints, eight others have been beatified and declared "blessed." A preparatory step. Something for you to work at, Charlie.

CHARLIE. Yes, Colonel.

GOLDMAN. When you die, Charlie . . . when you die . . . it's a condition in my Will everything you leave goes to the first Jewish Pope. The first Jewish American Pope. You follow? To be held in perpetuity . . . if necessary. You follow?

CHARLIE. Yes.

GOLDMAN. That would be something, wouldn't it, Charlie? The first Jewish American Pope.

CHARLIE. Pope Hymie.

GOLDMAN. (*Surprised.*) I didn't know you were a wit!

CHARLIE. I'm not.

GOLDMAN. Everything's a matter of practice, keep at it. (*Crossing L.*) The fish ain't happy.

CHARLIE. Perhaps they smell the snow.

GOLDMAN. (*Crosses D. L. of love seat.*) You're sensitive. Of course, this guy Dorff might just be eliminated. That's my worry. You see . . . I've done all my research. I've got my case. (*Pause.*) They say the word's around town I'm thinkin' of suicide.

CHARLIE. (*Astonished.*) I've certainly not heard that, Mr. Goldman.

GOLDMAN. Colonel, Charlie, Colonel. Yeah, they say I carry poison. They got a great museum in Prague— seventy thousand dead names painted on the walls . . . couple of hundred years and my . . . effort . . . might be in vain. Only Israel left.

CHARLIE. How'd you mean, Colonel?

GOLDMAN. (*Sits on love seat.*) The final assimilation. What the council said, Charlie . . . what the Pope's council said was: "The Jewish people should never be presented as one rejected, cursed, or guilty of deicide, and the council deplores and condemns hatred and persecution

of Jews whether they arose in former or in our own days."
Overwhelming majority! Ain't that ironic?

(*The HOUSE-PHONE rings.* CHARLIE *takes it.*)

CHARLIE. What? All right, I'll tell him. (CHARLIE *puts
down the phone.*) Mr. Goldman, Pete says two men are
sitting across the street in a Cadillac and like you said he
was to tell you if he thought anyone was watching the
apartment.

(*Pause.*)

GOLDMAN. Did he say what kind of men?
CHARLIE. Two young men.

(*Pause.*)

GOLDMAN. (*Rises, crosses to desk.*) I gotta think about
this. (*Pause.*) Life goes so fast. I pulled down seven of
my own constructions last year. Seven of my own build-
ings—I pulled 'em down. (*Pause.*) Tell Pete to describe
'em. (*Sits.*) Without letting them see him tell him to
describe 'em.
CHARLIE. (*He picks up the phone.*) Pete. Mr. Goldman
says don't let 'em see you but what do they look like?
(*Pause.*) Both young, one blond, Mr. Goldman.
GOLDMAN. They got hats on?
CHARLIE. Hats? No.
GOLDMAN. No, I don't think they wear hats. (*Pause.*)
You say one's blond?
CHARLIE. Yes.
GOLDMAN. They're not Arabs then?
CHARLIE. Could they be Arabs, Pete? (*Pause.*) Pete
doesn't think they're Arabs.
GOLDMAN. German?
CHARLIE. German, Pete? (*Pause.*) Maybe, Mr. Gold-
man.

GOLDMAN. Colonel, Charlie, Colonel. Between you and me it's Colonel. Charlie, tell Pete to come to a conclusion, for Chrissake.

CHARLIE. Come to a conclusion, for Chrissake. (*Pause.*) He says he can't, Colonel.

GOLDMAN. Okay.

(CHARLIE *hangs up and crosses to* C.)

CHARLIE. Why don't we call the police?

GOLDMAN. Can't do that. Don't want nobody shot. (*Pause.*) Hey, there's a guy in Carolina upset. Goddam Jewish father's gotta boy actin' Jesus Christ in the School Nativity. Boy won't give up the part. Says it's a great role. (CHARLIE *crosses* U. C. *and looks out.*) I got an idea from that. There's all kind of sick Semitics in these shtetls, Charlie. They got these cardiac Jews, that's Jewish-in-the-heart Jews, they got these revolvin' door Jews, that's in-at-Rosh-Hashannah-out-on-Yom-Kippur-Jews, they got these South-African-keep-silent-about-apartheid Jews . . . and they got these suicide Jews. They got *them* all over. So fill in *my* grave, Charlie.

CHARLIE. (*Crossing down to* L. *of desk.*) I thought you wanted to be cremated, Colonel.

GOLDMAN. (*Laughs.*) Yeah, put me in one of my own incinerators. Can't make any difference. However . . . however, that matter may soon be out of my hands. (*Pause.*) I don't know if they're enemies or friends, you see. (*Pause.*) Jesus, I hopè I'm right to do this. (*Pause.*) I'd like to see your new suits. Give my love to your Momma . . . that's a word . . . it's a word that I don't use too often . . . L . . . O . . . V . . . E. And I never speak of the children. Examine the will. It'll please you, Charlie. (*Pause. The TELEPHONE rings.* GOLDMAN *answers it.*) Yeah? (GOLDMAN *puts the phone down. Looking ironically upward as he rises.*) Okay, J.C.! Go down there and invite 'em up.

CHARLIE. What?

GOLDMAN. (*Crosses to* CHARLIE.) I want 'em all up here, my little lanzman.

CHARLIE. I can't, Mr. Goldman.

GOLDMAN. Charlie, Charlie, I got the cash.

CHARLIE. I can't, Mr. Goldman. I'm too frightened.

GOLDMAN. Do you want me to change my will? Tell 'em I have to find peace with my former enemies. They'll believe that. Tell 'em it's for the youth of Germany. They'll believe that too. Until I offer them the cash! I got the cash, I *got* the cash, I got the loot.

CHARLIE. All right, Mr. Goldman.

GOLDMAN. Quick as you can, Charlie.

(CHARLIE COHN *leaves in the ELEVATOR.* GOLDMAN *opens the vault door.* GOLDMAN *drops his pistol in the fish tank. Takes a capsule from the desk and puts it in his mouth. Then goes to the Hi-Fi, smiles, puts on a BRASS-BAND "Rosamunda." Sits down again. The ELEVATOR rises. Out of the elevator come* TWO YOUNG MEN, *guns in their hands, followed by* CHARLIE COHN *and* MRS. ROSEN. MRS. ROSEN *has her gun in* CHARLIE COHN's *back.*)

MRS. ROSEN. Turn that off. (CHARLIE *pushes the T.V. by mistake, then shuts off the HI-FI.*) Sit down. (CHARLIE *sits* D. L.) Search the place.

(STEIGER *goes out of the hall,* DURER *into the locked room.* CHARLIE COHN *sits trembling.* MRS. ROSEN *points her gun at* GOLDMAN.)

GOLDMAN. I'm not armed, kid. Gave my gun to the fish.

MRS. ROSEN. On your knees.

GOLDMAN. Don't talk to *me* like that, Rosy Rosen.

MRS. ROSEN. So you know me?

GOLDMAN. Of you. *Of* you, Rosy.

MRS. ROSEN. Then it's mutual. Tell me a joke.

GOLDMAN. Born in Brooklyn. Didn't like the President. Didn't like Roosevelt. Emigrated. Emigrated to Tel Aviv.

(*Silence.* STEIGER *comes back.*)

STEIGER. No one else here.

MRS. ROSEN. Check him. (DURER *comes out of the locked room.*) What's in there?

DURER. A stool. A table. Cartons of chocolate bars. And a copy of "Mein Kampf."

GOLDMAN. How much?

MRS. ROSEN. What?

GOLDMAN. How much?

MRS. ROSEN. What for?

GOLDMAN. For my life.

MRS. ROSEN. (*Smiling.*) Not Christ's blood would buy it. Not from me. I can't think what you heard.

GOLDMAN. (*Slowly.*) But I understood . . . one million dollars . . . one million dollars cash. Three. Three million dollars cash. Give me a few days and I'll make it seven. Seven million dollars hard cash. (*A pause.*) There's been a mistake.

(*The* TWO YOUNG MEN *search* GOLDMAN. *They take off his shirt. They examine, they poke.*)

STEIGMAN. Peh! Peh! (DURER *hits* GOLDMAN *in the stomach and* GOLDMAN *spits out the capsule.* STEIGER *picks it up off the floor.*) Phial of poison.

MRS. ROSEN. Lift up his left arm.

STEIGER. Scar!

MRS. ROSEN. Insignia and blood type tattooed under that scar, Mr. Cohn.

CHARLIE. Insignia of what?

MRS. ROSEN. S.S. Insignia.

(STEIGER *runs his fingers over* GOLDMAN'S *collar bone and* GOLDMAN'S *left kneecap.*)

STEIGER. Two old fractures—same places as the X-rays.

(MRS. ROSEN *takes a photograph out of the briefcase, studies it, nods her head.*)

MRS. ROSEN. What's his cap size?

DURER. Twenty-two.

MRS. ROSEN. Bring him here. (STEIGER *shoves him to the desk.* DURER *twists his hand.* GOLDMAN *falls on his knees.* MRS. ROSEN *stares down at* GOLDMAN.) You are Adolf Karl Dorff.

CHARLIE. Dorff!

MRS. ROSEN. You are Adolf Karl Dorff.

GOLDMAN. Eight million dollars hard cash.

MRS. ROSEN. If you cooperate you will be given a fair trial and the benefit of legal counsel.

GOLDMAN. Don't you understand it's cash?

CHARLIE. You are Israelis then?

MRS. ROSEN. If you do not cooperate I will shoot you here.

CHARLIE. Where will you take him?

MRS. ROSEN. He was a Colonel in the Einsatzgruppen, the mobile killing unit of the S.S.

CHARLIE. What did he do?

MRS. ROSEN. The court will decide that.

(GOLDMAN *rises.*)

GOLDMAN. I am an American citizen.

MRS. ROSEN. We have discussed that.

GOLDMAN. I am a citizen of the United States.

MRS. ROSEN. We have discussed that.

GOLDMAN. The United States will not permit the violation of its sovereignty.

MRS. ROSEN. There's already been a precedent.

GOLDMAN. That's different. That wasn't in the United States.

MRS. ROSEN. So you want to be shot?

GOLDMAN. Murderer.

MRS. ROSEN. I have my orders.

GOLDMAN. (*Crossing to* C.) Orders! Orders! I had my orders! (GOLDMAN *draws himself up. Thunders.*) What are the demands of justice? What are the demands of law? (*Pause.*) Who are my judges? And by what right? (*Pause. Calmly.*) I will go with you. I will go with you, sheep. Yes, I'll tell you a joke, Rosy Rosen, I'll tell you a couple of jokes and I'll bleed you that blood you're talkin' about.

CURTAIN

ACT TWO

A cell. Outside the peephole a GUARD; *inside* DURER *on a stool,* MRS. ROSEN *on a chair, and* GOLDMAN *on the bed. It is hot.* GOLDMAN *is dressed in prison clothes. Silence.*

MRS. ROSEN. (*Rises, crosses* U. C.) In the reports of the Einsatzgruppen I notice plain words do not occur: we have "final solution," "evacuation," and "special treatment." On the other hand, in *your* reports you always stated "extermination" or "killing." Why is that?

GOLDMAN. (*Rises to her.*) Always call a spade a spade. Those euphemisms you speak of were best for keepin' order—they didn't want the typists to get the message— you follow? But in my case I'm not here to tell you I didn't enjoy it—I'm here to tell you I did. (GOLDMAN *laughs.*) No clerk, Rosen! Issued my own orders, plotted my own plots, had a ball. You follow?

MRS. ROSEN. Why did you pretend to be Jewish?

GOLDMAN. Have you noticed I'm losin' weight? Much fitter. It was all that rich food done me in. And I am sleepin' great. I *am* sleepin' great. You should come in and join me. Come in and diet. Come in and lay yourself down and diet.

MRS. ROSEN. Why did you pretend to be Jewish?

GOLDMAN. I'm not here to plead I took orders. I had initiative. First honest man who's stood in your dock. Like you got the Fuehrer himself in here. (*Indicating tape recorder.*) That a German machine? That a Grundig?

MRS. ROSEN. Japanese.

GOLDMAN. Great people for trade, your lot. Rosy, you wear too much make-up.

MRS. ROSEN. Why did you pretend to be Jewish?

35

GOLDMAN. Always had a sense of humor. I'm concerned about your make-up, madam, concerned about your maquillage, you're beginnin' to attract me.

MRS. ROSEN. (*She sits in chair.*) Are you Jewish?

GOLDMAN. (*Sits on the bed, facing* ROSEN.) I bet you people got troubles with the Americans by now.

MRS. ROSEN. Why do you say that?

GOLDMAN. I'm a citizen of the United States. I know you've got troubles with the Americans by now. They won't waive sovereign rights so easily. I know that. I know the American nation.

MRS. ROSEN. Why did you pretend to be Jewish?

GOLDMAN. I might demand an International Court. I might just get that. I have a lot of acquaintances. I'm sayin' you should go on a diet.

MRS. ROSEN. We won't give you up.

GOLDMAN. No? I got the funds. I have the loot. Brooklyn, I'm sayin' you eat too much.

MRS. ROSEN. The world will learn to understand that we will never give you up.

GOLDMAN. (*Gently.*) Don't be so goddamned arrogant. Don't be so goddamned Israeli. Not with me. I'm no clerk. I ain't got guilt. I'm not riddled and weary. I'm an American. I'm still an American. To keep me here you'll need my help.

MRS. ROSEN. How do you mean?

GOLDMAN. (*Lies back on the bed.*) That's all for the day— I gotta work it out.

MRS. ROSEN. (*Sits above* GOLDMAN *on the bed.*) Are you Jewish?

GOLDMAN. (*Sitting up.*) Am I an encyclopaedia? I'm human . . . that's what I am. There's too many definitions around here. Do I wear a yomulka?

MRS. ROSEN. Why did you pretend to be Jewish?

GOLDMAN. (*Laughing.*) A woman of your age, you should wear no make-up at all. Three corselets but no maquillage. I got nothin' against you personal, sweetheart, but the way you go round, you're a dog. (*Pause.* MRS.

ROSEN *gazes at him, smiles, leaves the cell with* DURER. *A* GUARD *enters and sits watching* GOLDMAN.) That woman Rosen eats too much. She's what they call a compulsive. Mind you I always like Kosher. We got a restaurant in New York killed more Hebrews than I did. (*Rises, crosses* U. C.) I'm sexin' her up for the Court . . . you follow? (*Silence.*) Of course I like a bit of pork now and again. They keep askin' me if I'm Jewish. I don't know what that word means. (*He stands at the foot of the bed.*)

(*Silence. The LIGHT turns to morning.* MRS. ROSEN *enters the cell with* STEIGER. *The* GUARD *goes out.*)

MRS. ROSEN. Good morning Colonel Dorff. (*Sits in the chair.*)
GOLDMAN. Good morning, sexy, have a good breakfast?

(STEIGER *switches on the TAPE RECORDER.*)

MRS. ROSEN. Why did you pretend to be Jewish?
GOLDMAN. If it should be proved . . . I mean proved that I gave false information when I became a citizen of the United States . . . now that would help you with the Americans. But I know you can't prove that, sexy.
MRS. ROSEN. How do you know we can't prove it?
GOLDMAN. (*Laughing.*) I believe you were asking me why I pretended to be Jewish. Are you Jewish?
MRS. ROSEN. How do you know we can't prove you gave false information when you applied to become a citizen of the United States, Colonel Dorff?
GOLDMAN. Are *you* Jewish, Rose? (*Pause. Sits.*) I pretended to be Jewish because I made the acquaintance of old-American-Jewish-Uncle-Hymie's nephew, Arthur Goldman. Got to know him in Deutschland. Got to know Arthur so well I called him "cousin." Perhaps he was, cousin.
MRS. ROSEN. He is dead?

GOLDMAN. Don't you know that?

MRS. ROSEN. Who killed Arthur Goldman?

GOLDMAN. Between you and me the question is who didn't kill Arthur Goldman.

MRS. ROSEN. Did you kill Arthur Goldman?

GOLDMAN. I have brooded on that. I have pondered on that. (*Pause. Rises and crosses* U. C.) Get this while you can, fatty: (*Takes mike from* STEIGER.) I the undersigned. Yeah, that's it. I the undersigned Adolf Karl Dorff, declared of my own free will, dear President Johnson, and dear people and government of the United States, that it has become clear to me there is no point in hiding any more. I declare I came to Israel of my own free will and am willing to stay here and face an authorized court. I understand I will be given legal aid but I am going to decline it because I want to present such a case as will interest the new generation. I make this statement without threats of any kind. Since I cannot always remember details I hereby ask to be assisted by having access to certain documents. Finally I reserve the right to know what witnesses the State of Israel will call to defend my-self, and to wear my uniform—Colonel, S.S.—in the Court.

MRS. ROSEN. I shall have to consult my superiors.

GOLDMAN. Not to be signed unless all the conditions fulfilled. I shall want my uniform brushed and pressed. And my jackboots gleaming. (MRS. ROSEN *sighs, leaves the cell with* STEIGER. *The* GUARD *enters the cell.* GOLDMAN *goes to sit in the shaft of sunlight. Takes off his shirt and sunbathes. He grins at the* GUARD.) Gotta get a good tan for the court. D'you love your momma? (GOLDMAN *lies on the bed.*) I remember my palaces, kid. I wander through their rooms. I'm the last of the lions, me and my Sienese primitives. You should have seen my country place with my wife Matilda. She was no fatso. Matilda was a princess. Me and Matilda walk with long-legged dogs down the great terraces and enter her bedroom through the window. I seize her beneath the Pom-

peian frescoes and I hurl her upon the four-poster.
Matilda was delighted. A great American gal! "What, no
petting?" she cried. Lemon tea, cognac and sweet cakes,
and when she came she cried like an angel, seventy-two
times in a single night. Oh, how my Matilda restored me.
Forgive me, fella, it's the heat. Matilda was a princess,
you see. For some reason . . . for some reason, I bought
her Rembrandts, I bought her Rubens, I bought her Van
Dycks, I bought her Canalettos, I bought her Raphaels
and because she had Botticelli eyes I bought her Botticelli.
Matilda. I give her a bit of everything, faience, maiolica,
ceramics. A little Russian tapestry, a little Greek coral, a
little Louis Quatorze to sit on, and a little Madonna, for
she was religious. When she died she wept, and I lived on
in Manhattan. She was very ill, she lived on the edge of
a scalpel. Should have got my pistol out and shot her in
the head, but I couldn't do it. With her, my Matilda, I
was sentimental. I loved my Gentile wife, Matilda. My
second wife, you understand. (*Pause.*) My first wife was
a child-bearer. She bore me a litter. Yes, she bore me a
brood. It's not that I never sowed my seed. (*He rises,
puts on his shirt, and stands* C.)

(*The LIGHT changes to dawn.* MRS. ROSEN *enters the
cell with* DURER, *carrying a document and newspapers. The* GUARD *goes out.*)

MRS. ROSEN. Your guarantee, signed by us. And pub-
lished in the newspapers.
GOLDMAN. (*Takes papers and sits on bed.*) You got it
in the Tribune?
MRS. ROSEN. Of course.
GOLDMAN. London Times?
MRS. ROSEN. Of course. (MRS. ROSEN *flicks her fingers*— STEIGER *enters with Goldman's uniform.* GOLDMAN
salutes. STEIGER *puts it on the chair.* MRS. ROSEN *sits on
the bed.*) How did you manage to convince Hymie Goldman that you were his nephew, Arthur?

GOLDMAN. Family likeness. Got it in Pravda?

MRS. ROSEN. D'you mean you were related?

GOLDMAN. Cousins. All cousins. My Aunt Judith and my momma Sarah. Got it in Der Spiegel?

MRS. ROSEN. So are you Jewish, Colonel Dorff?

GOLDMAN. All I had to do was convince old American sentimental-isolationist-blind-bespectacled-deaf-as-a-post-in-one-ear-not-doing-too-good-at-the-time-capital-after-wards-by-me-trebled-old-Uncle-Manhattan-guilt-ridden-Jewish-Hymie.

MRS. ROSEN. Are you therefore, Adolf Karl Dorff—one-time Colonel in the Einsatzgruppen—are you, Colonel, Jewish?

GOLDMAN. (*Rises, crosses to* c.) Hear this. (GOLDMAN *takes off his shirt and trousers, begins to dress in the uniform of an S.S. Colonel.*) Can't be too specific. Don't want to ball up my case. (*Pause.*) Am I Jewish? I tell you this—my father was Group A. A hundred and three now. Still doing great. One of the oldest guys in Germany. Cousin of Hindenburg's. The Fuehrer never forgot that. Am I Jewish? My dear madam, it was I. G. Farben who discovered the site. Very suitable for synthetic coal-oil and rubber. I entered the place laughing—my first mission of that kind—they handed over their valuables and outer clothing—I put 'em in the anti-tank ditch, I lay 'em down flat. I shot 'em through the nape of the neck, personal, gaining confidence at every pull. Sent in my report. Very honest report. Never slept better in my life. What with me and my father, I did great. Momma was forgot. They put her in the closet. One day later, in the pink, in the prime of life I came to a pit. Outside Dubno, Poland. Getting quite cold round there. I saw one thousand pairs of shoes and five hundred pairs of panties. Nobody was complaining or asking for mercy. Sheep. One old grandmother, bald as a coot, should have worn a wig, picks up a baby: the baby laughs, the father laughs, the mother laughs. They all look up at the sky, including the baby. And a girl, a girl points down to her pubics and she tells me she's twenty years old. You follow? So I walk over to the mount, I get to the grave. "Wedge 'em in," I said, laughing. Am I Jewish? We light cigarettes and we start the shooting. We fill up the bottom. They lay in from the top. The blood runs down from their heads. They lay in from the sides. We pack 'em more, and underneath, there's movement. Waving arms and suchlike. Naked they go down the steps, they climb on the heads of the people below and I tell 'em exactly where. I'm a great packer—should have made trunks. Am I Jewish? They lay on top of their dead or dying and we shot, shot, shot. I never missed one. So the last lot lay on the pyre so high we reached up from the sides and give it at arm's length. Just a day in my life. Just a clear day to enjoy forever. Am I Jewish? I don't know about my mother, but my father was pure-blooded Aryan. That I'm proud of.

(GOLDMAN *laughs and laughs*. MRS. ROSEN *waits*.)

MRS. ROSEN. Tell me about your first wife, Colonel.

GOLDMAN. (*Indignantly*.) Jesus! You don't seem to appreciate the pleasure I got! Very lovely, my first wife. My German wife, Marlene. Another princess. The Fuehrer said: "You gotta great gal there, Addy." I called him Addy. He called *me* Addy. The Fuehrer said: "The man who misjudges and disregards the racial laws actually forfeits the happiness that seems to be his."

MRS. ROSEN. No children, Colonel?

GOLDMAN. That was sad, Momma.

MRS. ROSEN. What was sad?

GOLDMAN. Lost touch. Lost touch.

MRS. ROSEN. Could we find them for you, Colonel?

GOLDMAN. Not a chance. (*Pause*.) Spare *me* a moment of grief, madam.

MRS. ROSEN. Is it a point of your inner life—a certain feeling of guilt?

GOLDMAN. Jesus. You sound like a tourist guide. The Fuehrer wanted it—it was great to go along. And I got such cooperation from your folks. Your folks always made up the transport lists. The chosen, was chosen, and well they chose! You get it? (*Sits on the bed.*) What about you and me layin' down to it, sweetheart? What about you and me producin'? What about a brand new 1965 German-Jewish swaddler? (*Pause.*) I think you got the milk. I think you could nurse him. (GOLDMAN *smiles at her.*)

(STEIGER *crosses slowly to above* GOLDMAN.)

MRS. ROSEN. No thank you, Colonel Dorff.
GOLDMAN. (*Rising. Briskly.*) My boots.
MRS. ROSEN. One moment. (*Rises.*) You have a visitor.

(*She signs to* STEIGER *who exits.*)

GOLDMAN. A what?
MRS. ROSEN. (*She laughs.*) Your only friend . . . the one person in the whole world who has asked to testify *for* you.
GOLDMAN. *For* me?
MRS. ROSEN. *For* you.

(*Pause.*)

GOLDMAN. I don't want no testifyin'. I'll do my own testifyin'. (*Pause.*) Who? Who is it? Who've you exhumed, Rosy? Who have you taken that spade to? (*Pause.*) You got me nervous, Rosy.

(*They wait. Dressed in his new suit,* CHARLIE COHN *enters the cell.*)

CHARLIE. Hello, Mr. Goldman.
GOLDMAN. Charlie! Charlie, Charlie, Charlie! You had me nervous, Charlie. You got me sweatin'! I thought you was a contemporary.

CHARLIE. It's very good to see you, Mr. Goldman.

GOLDMAN. It's very good to see you, Charlie. You look great. Just great. (CHARLIE COHN *puts out his hand.* GOLDMAN *takes it in both of his.* GOLDMAN *pumps* CHARLIE COHN's *hand up and down in his own.*) Boy you look a million dollars! Ten years younger. Don't say another word until we get the old bag outta' here.

MRS. ROSEN. (*She laughs again.*) See you in court, Mr. Cohn.

(MRS. ROSEN *and* DURER *leave. The* GUARD *enters.*)

STEIGER. Mish Marim! (*He slams the door. Pause.*)

GOLDMAN. What did the tailor charge for the suit?

CHARLIE. Four hundred.

GOLDMAN. Four hundred. Four hundred dollars! Who did he send the bill to?

CHARLIE. You, Mr. Goldman.

GOLDMAN. (*He smiles, begins to laugh.*) There's something very funny about that, Charlie. And two of 'em. Two of 'em at four hundred. And what about the vicuna! (GOLDMAN *laughs and laughs.*)

CHARLIE. But you did say he should, Mr. Goldman. I remember that distinctly.

GOLDMAN. (*Rubbing his eyes and helpless.*) None of you guys lost your heads. None of you fellas lost your sense of proportion. I'm proud of you, Charlie.

(GOLDMAN *indicates the chair and* CHARLIE *sits.* GOLD-MAN *sits on bed. Pause.*)

CHARLIE. I read your statement in the papers.

GOLDMAN. The Tribune?

CHARLIE. No, the Times. The Tribune's on its way out, Mr. Goldman. I only take the Times now. It was a very nice photograph. (*Pause.*) I see you've got your uniform on.

GOLDMAN. Yes.

CHARLIE. Uh-huh.

GOLDMAN. Do you like it?

CHARLIE. It's very smart.

GOLDMAN. It suits me, don't it?

CHARLIE. (*Pause.*) Have they been looking after you all right? Has the cooking been to your satisfaction? (*Rises to above bed.*) Now what about the bed? Have you been sleeping all right?

(*Pause.*)

GOLDMAN. How's my city? How's Manhattan?

CHARLIE. (*Sits on the stool.*) Worse than ever, Mr. Goldman. Terrible. Just terrible. You can't go into the Park now—even in the daylight. Sometimes I think to myself . . . I can't walk up this street. An' then you heard about the blackout.

GOLDMAN. No.

CHARLIE. Oh, yes; all the lights failed, all the lights went out.

GOLDMAN. How's the new Mayor?

CHARLIE. I can honestly report, Mr. Goldman, he is a very personable young man.

(*Pause.*)

GOLDMAN. And how's Momma?

CHARLIE. We are not speaking, Mr. Goldman. I was forced . . . I had to move out.

(*Pause.*)

GOLDMAN. Where you livin'?

CHARLIE. (*Sits in chair* L.) In the apartment. In the penthouse. I thought I had best move back there permanently and keep an eye on things.

GOLDMAN. (*Grinning.*) Thank you, Charlie.

CHARLIE. You see, Momma didn't want me to do that. And I must tell you she didn't want me to come over here. She did not want me to go into the court. She wanted me to disown you, Mr. Goldman.

GOLDMAN. Momma know about the will?

CHARLIE. No. Only me and the lawyers know about the will.

GOLDMAN. (*Rises to* U. C.) That Tailor know about the will?

CHARLIE. No. Nobody else, Mr. Goldman.

GOLDMAN. You thought that best.

CHARLIE. Oh, yes.

GOLDMAN. (*Sits on the stool.*) What will you do with it all, Charlie?

CHARLIE. (*Rises to him.*) Well I—I would just go on with it. I would just expand. I would be very prudent, very careful. I would employ the best men. But I do have lots of ideas of my own for the decorating.

GOLDMAN. I guess you'll take over all of the decoratin' side yourself—all of the interior decoratin'.

CHARLIE. Yes, I think I will do that, Mr. Goldman. Yes, I do have that in mind.

(*Pause.*)

GOLDMAN. What . . . what are you gonna say in the court, Charlie? What do you have in mind for the court?

CHARLIE. I just want to tell them how good you've been to me, Mr. Goldman—and to everybody.

GOLDMAN. Were you thinkin' of telling them about the will?

CHARLIE. No, I hadn't thought to do that.

GOLDMAN. *That* hasn't crossed your mind?

CHARLIE. No, Mr. Goldman.

GOLDMAN. (*He laughs and laughs.*) I love ya, Charlie.

CHARLIE. (*Smiling.*) Thank you, Mr. Goldman.

GOLDMAN. I chose the right man.

(*Long pause.*)

CHARLIE. Mr. Goldman . . . why have you left *me* your money? (*Silence.*) I mean why have you left all your money to a Jew, Mr. Goldman?

(*Pause.*)

GOLDMAN. Because I love you, Charlie—you know that. (GOLDMAN *stares at* CHARLIE.) Come here. (CHARLIE *goes to* GOLDMAN. GOLDMAN *waits until* CHARLIE *gets close, then whacks* CHARLIE *across the face.* CHARLIE *staggers back, sits on the bed, bursts into tears. Very quietly.*) Stay out of the court. Don't come in there and ball me up. (*He goes over to* CHARLIE.) There's more to this than my future. There's more to this than my palaces. (GOLDMAN *steps back, calls to* DURER.) My boots.

(*A* GUARD *enters.* GUARD *gives* GOLDMAN *the boots.* GOLDMAN *stamps into them.* GOLDMAN *and* DURER *leave the cell.*)

BLACKOUT

(*The* PROSECUTOR'S *voice on microphone speaks in the blackout.*)

PROSECUTOR'S VOICE. How could it happen? Why did it happen? What of the Allies? Why the Germans? And why the Jews? I tell you only a Jewish court will render justice to Jews; I tell you it is our duty to sit in judgment on our enemies, I tell you it is our right. But I make no ethnic distinctions— I would indict this man for crimes against other peoples if crimes there were—but this man . . . this monster . . . has concerned himself with Jews, is only concerned with Jews. This monster has only murdered Jews! And when I look at this monster *I* am only concerned with Jews. (*The LIGHTS come on.*) You will hear Jewish witness after Jewish witness, Jewish suffering

after Jewish suffering. Yes, I will show you the calamity
of the Jewish people in this generation; yes, I will show
you the calamity of Jewry; yes, I will show you what we
suffered, and I will show you why. Because . . . because
the whole tragedy of Jewry is to be my central concern.
(*The* PROSECUTOR *sits down.*)

(*During the blackout, the cell has changed into a court.*
GOLDMAN *enters with a* GUARD, *who puts him into
the booth.* GOLDMAN *sits in a bullet-proof glass
booth; The* PRESIDING JUDGE *at a table; The* PROS-
ECUTOR *at another;* MRS. ROSEN, STEIGER *and*
DURER *at another.*)

GOLDMAN. Excuse me.

JUDGE. Yes.

GOLDMAN. Having heard with admiration for many
days the magniloquence of the Prosecutor . . . having
listened to his many points . . . his many intentions . . .
may I make a personal observation? I mean . . . not
knowing your Israeli legal procedure precisely, not wishing
to disturb it—I just ask. What I mean *is,* Your Honor—
it's obvious you got to be Orthodox around here.

JUDGE. What kind of personal observations?

GOLDMAN. Eh?

JUDGE. What kind of personal observations?

GOLDMAN. Been put off my stroke. (*He points to the
audience.*) Just seen Mrs. Dorff out there. Jesus. She's
blond. And they told me she was dead. My German wife,
you understand, Marlene. Excuse me, Your Honor. Call
me a bigamist. Bit of a shock. Changed her name, I
shouldn't wonder. Wearing a wig, I don't doubt. (*He grins
at* MRS. ROSEN.) Don't get jealous, Rosy—that's all over
and done with.

JUDGE. Adolf Karl Dorff—

GOLDMAN. Rosy's a .jealous woman! "That's one thing
I'll never forgive," she said. That's what you said, didn't
you, Rosy? Hi, Mrs. Dorff. Hi, Marlene.

JUDGE. Adolf Karl Dorff, what kind of personal observation?

GOLDMAN. Please don't shout, Your Honor. It echoes in here. If I get frightened I might revert. All the time I've got to watch that. It's about the indictment.

JUDGE. Specific to the indictment?

GOLDMAN. No, very general.

JUDGE. Then your turn will come in its proper time.

GOLDMAN. Who's gonna decide that?

JUDGE. The Court will decide that. Don't provoke me.

GOLDMAN. I'm sorry, Your Honor. I'm sorry, I didn't mean to do that. That's not my intention, but the point is, Your Honor, you know your local rules and I don't. Except on times when I'm directly answering Jewish questions, I think I should be able to put up my Gentile hand and ask you if I can make a Gentile observation. I mean what are we interested in here, Your Honor, justice or the suffering of the Jewish people?

JUDGE. I shall decide that. Very well. I shall rule on each observation.

GOLDMAN. Thank you, Your Honor. (*To* MRS. ROSEN.) Rosy, you might tell Marlene, I saw her friend in Manhattan and he was looking just great.

JUDGE. Keep to the indictment, Dorff.

GOLDMAN. Excuse me . . . the mind wanders . . . Your Honor, when your prosecutor comes in, comes in from her press conferences, and getting on the T.V.— which I didn't—and makes her very magniloquent jerk-you-in-the-tear-ball speeches—and has been raising questions of suffering and how could all this have happened, and why did it happen to the Jews, and what was everybody else doin', and why did we Germans do it so bad and so on and so forth? Now these are very great questions: but if I understand justice, Your Honor, it's nobody's suffering that should be on trial here, it's what I done. It's what I did. It's what I did that's the point. Did I not hear, Your Honor, the prosecutor conclude her opening speech by "the whole tragedy of Jewry is to be our central concern"?

JUDGE. You did hear that.

GOLDMAN. But I, I, Your Honor, *I* am your central concern.

JUDGE. Yes, yes. I shall make you my concern.

GOLDMAN. Thank you, Your Honor. May I point out somethin' else?

JUDGE. Yes.

GOLDMAN. I saved your two young Jewish guys and Mrs. Rosen, my interrogator, murder; Charlie Cohn invites them into my Manhattan apartment and what would they have done if I'd refused to accompany them out? Is that not such a crime as you would call my own? Would not the pistol have been at the back of my head?

JUDGE. Irrelevant.

GOLDMAN. But I mean what's got to be proved, Your Honor—that I'm not fit to live?

JUDGE. From now on when you digress, I shall switch your microphone off.

GOLDMAN. Judge, you're honest! I appreciate ya!

(MRS. LEVI *enters the stand.*)

MRS. LEVI. Levi. Forty-seven people were led barefoot to the quarry. Dorff stood at the bottom of the steps watching his men load jagged boulders on their backs, then these people had to carry them to the top of the cliff. Each journey the boulders grew heavier. In the evening, forty bodies were lying along the road.

GOLDMAN. Yes, I remember that, but *you* did great—remarkable constitution. Course, some of you might be wonderin' why Mrs. Levi and her head friends got on the train in the first place—got on the train to the quarry. There was only three guards, as I recall—Kirlewanger's got a villa in Cairo, I'm here, and Pohse's drawing a pension in Hamburg—anyway, why did all these people keep gettin' on cattle trains and goin' to quarries and suchlike? Might I enlighten you on that, Your Honor?

JUDGE. No, I know why. Their fate was beyond their knowledge. Every conjecture was arbitrary. They had no foundation.

GOLDMAN. Yes, that's it. I always confused 'em. Everything was done so simple. Ask for your suitcase, I said: "Sure, later!" Ask for your baby, I said: "Sure, stick with the kid." All very peaceful, all very calm. Of course if I had to make an example I'd use my imagination—stuff your genitals in your mouth, burn your feet off . . . somethin' like that. Couldn't allow any precedents. Couldn't allow any heroes . . . you follow? (*Silence. MRS. LEVI leaves the stand. An OLD MAN enters.*) What I don't get, Your Honor, is why the prosecutor does not demand the exposure of all the German authorities who permitted me to get on with my German work, and all those Jews who helped me? I got West German names here of civil servants, businessmen, ministers, priests, doctors, lawyers, generals, whores and housefraus . . . Here we are in alphabetical order: Mr. I. G. Braun, former ministerialat . . .

PROSECUTOR. I object— Not admissible evidence.

JUDGE. Sustained.

OLD MAN. Marowski. The Star of Bethlehem reached down and radiated life into my inert body. I opened my eyes and gazed . . .

(*But GOLDMAN flings open the door of the glass booth.*)

GOLDMAN. This man is a nut.

OLD MAN. (*Shouts.*) The Star of Bethlehem, a power above nature, reached down into my inert body and radiated . . .

GOLDMAN. (*Crosses to stand. Shouts.*) Shut your mouth or I'll have you shot!

JUDGE. Take the prisoner back! (*GOLDMAN turns.*) I will not have you intimidating the witnesses. (*GOLDMAN starts back, then halts and stamps his feet.*) Colonel Dorff! Lock the prisoner in the booth!

(*The* GUARDS *do so. The* OLD MAN *bursts into tears and is helped from the stand.*)

GOLDMAN. (*He goes back toward the booth, but stops and looks at the audience.*) What's happened to Marlene? You done away with her, Rosy?

MRS. ROSEN. May I answer this?

JUDGE. Yes.

MRS. ROSEN. Mrs. Dorff does not wish to give evidence. She is returning to her . . . family and children in Bonn.

GOLDMAN. (*Clapping his hands.*) Very wise. Faithful wife, you see. Like a Hebrew wife. Like Brooklyn Rosy would be.

(GOLDMAN *goes back into the booth. A* YOUNG MAN *enters the stand.* GOLDMAN *reappears out of the booth.*)

YOUNG MAN. Tzelniker.

GOLDMAN. (*Shouts.*) You South African Jewish?

YOUNG MAN. Yes.

GOLDMAN. You live in Johannesburg?

YOUNG MAN. Yes.

GOLDMAN. Doin' well?

YOUNG MAN. Yes. I am doing very well.

GOLDMAN. No further questions.

JUDGE. (*To witness.*) Continue.

YOUNG MAN. Adolf Dorff is a murderer. On May 7th, 1942 he shot my mother and father before my eyes. That is all I have to say.

(*Within the booth,* GOLDMAN *is seen to clap. The* YOUNG MAN *leaves the witness stand. Another witness,* MR. LANDAU, *enters.*)

LANDAU. Landau. To be truthful, on the journey when Dorff and his men transferred us from Dachau to Buchenwald, although the journey lasted just as long as the one when I went to Dachau—a journey on which very many were murdered—on this journey under Dorff no one actually was murdered.

GOLDMAN. This man is an idiot!

JUDGE. Dorff, I will only allow you to speak as long as you are respectful. (*He switches on* GOLDMAN'S *MICRO-PHONE.*)

GOLDMAN. Excuse me, Your Honor. 'Course, nobody was murdered on that second journey. No need for it. The method! Can't you follow the method? That first journey was an initiation and an initiation's a project. An initiation's a defilement. Make 'em kick each other, make 'em accuse each other, make 'em curse their God, make 'em speak of their wives' intercourse and their own. Make 'em do it with their wives, make 'em do it with other wives, make 'em do it with children. After that they'll do anythin'—no need to waste your energy twice. And I always swore in the anal sphere. They always had to get permission to defecate. "Jewish prisoner number six million and a half most obediently prays to be permitted to defecate." What I was always looking out for, what I was always looking for when I was in the camps . . . were the survivors. What I sought was those not walking dead, those degraded and defiled but still human. I sought 'em with my pistol. And they were always different. They was cunning and tenacious. But I had an eye for 'em. I could smell 'em. They smelled of freedom. And I sought 'em out and I shot them because I could not let them live.

JUDGE. Thank you, Colonel Dorff.

GOLDMAN. One moment, Judge. One moment. I'm just warmin' up. You switch me off if I'm not respectful. Okay. So I've no need to mention names. Names! You can always get names. So we're all Jews. All Germans. And we all got names. Too *many names!* In the camps, fellas . . . you all got to be members of the Party. You follow? You got to be Nazis. All of you. You follow? Very few exceptions. You gotten to believe in our German superiority, you tortured your own traitors, you took our old uniforms,

you fixed 'em up, and you give us a snappy salute. You got
to love us. You follow? And as for the Pope. Don't think
he won't go back on all this dispensin'. Don't think he's
not got doctrinal and political considerations. Wait for the
usual pall of silence, fellas. They'll re-read the Gospels and
make another statement about the Pill. One of those four-
men commissions. And I am delighted, truly delighted that
the prosecutress does not hold the German people respon-
sible for the Fuehrer. The Prosecutor is a realist and great
for trade. The prosecutor drives a Volkswagen. But why
should we dwell on the past? What are these anti-semitic
daubings in London and Chicago? These desecrations in
Cologne? Deprivations in Russia? These publications in
Stockholm? And speaking of love, let me speak to you of
our beloved Fuehrer. Let me pay him tribute. People of
Israel. (GOLDMAN *looks at the* JUDGE *as if expecting to
be denied: calmly the* JUDGE *gazes at him. The* JUDGE
considers MRS. ROSEN, *then nods to* GOLDMAN, *who rises
with microphone.*) People of Jewry, let me speak to you
of my Fuehrer with love. (GOLDMAN *pauses. Very
quietly.*) He who answered our German need. He who
rescued us from the depths. His family background was
not distinguished, his education negligible. At the end of
that first World War not even a German citizen. To whom
did he appeal? To the people. His power lay in the love he
won from the people. When he spoke, at first he was shy,
he would hesitate, he would stammer, his body stiff, he
felt for his love like a blind man, the voice hushed, the
voice was flat, then the words came stronger, came
steadier, his body grew free, he would bang out his right
arm like a hammer, louder and louder he spoke, a torrent,
a waterfall, the climax was shouted and shouted, out and
up and beyond, and the end was absolute. Silence. Utter
silence. A great wide sweep of the right arm and so to the
tremendous cry, the vast overwhelming cry, the call of
love from the people. Deutschlanderwache. Heil Hitler.
Sieg Heil. Sieg Heil. Sieg Heil. Do I see you begin to
raise your hands? Do I hear you stamp your feet? He

gave us our history. He gave us our news, he gave us our art. He gave us our holidays, he gave us our leisure, and he gave our newly marrieds a copy of Mein Kampf. At the end we loved him. In Gotterdammerung we loved him. With the killers of the world at our throats, the hordes from the east and west, the capitalists and the communists, the bombers of cities, the murderers of our children, with bullets in our guts we loved him. Starving we loved him. With his head wobbling, his left arm slack, his hands a-tremble, we loved him. His generals lost him the war. His subordinates were unworthy. There was no successor. There was only him. Hess was mad, Goering reviled, Himmler rejected. He? He was loved. "Great King. Brave King. Wait yet a little while and the days of your suffering will be over. Already the sun of your good fortune stands behind the clouds and soon, beloved Fuehrer, soon this sun will rise upon you." He never deserted us. All but he! He, only, loved to the end. While he lived, Germany lived. And the people demanded it. We never denied him. People of Israel, we never denied him. And those who tell you different . . . lie. Those who tell you anything else, lie in their hearts. And if, if he were able to rise from the dead, he would prove it to you now. All over again. If only . . . if only we had someone to rise to . . . throw out our arms to . . . love . . . and stamp our feet for. Someone . . . someone to lead. (*Pause. Then calculatedly.*) People of Israel . . . people of Israel, if he had chosen you . . . if he had chosen *you* . . . *you* also would have followed where he led.

(*Pause. An* OLD WOMAN *rises in the front of the audience and says quietly:*)

OLD WOMAN. This man is not Dorff.
JUDGE. What's that?
OLD WOMAN. This man is not Dorff.
JUDGE. Not Dorff?
OLD WOMAN. This man is not Dorff. I must interrupt now because he is enjoying himself too much.

(*Silence. A* GUARD *moves towards the* OLD WOMAN.)

JUDGE. Wait! Wait a moment. I know this woman. Yes, . . . Come into the court. (PEOPLE *help the* OLD WOMAN *to the stand* [*Stage*]. GOLDMAN *sits motionless*.) Enter the stand, Mrs. Lehman.

(*The* WOMAN *enters the witness stand.*)

OLD WOMAN. I have sat and sat. Mr. Goldman was enlightening me. He made many points. Many, many points. But in the end I could not understand him. (GOLDMAN *puts down the mike*.) I knew him. I knew his cousin . . . Dorff. And I knew his wife and children. Mr. Goldman had three children. Teresa died on the train. Arthur and Jacob in the first year. Mrs. Goldman in the second. Christina. (*Pause.* GOLDMAN *sits.*) When Dorff came to our camp he would talk to this man and call him, "Cousin . . . ," "Cousin Arthur." Dorff would smile at this man, pat this man, give him food . . . so all could see. There was a likeness. A family likeness. I think Dorff must have been part Jewish or all Jewish. Dorff would come on Holy Days, give Mr. Goldman food and laugh. Mr. Goldman would wait till Dorff had gone, then give away the food. People followed Mr. Goldman. He never had enough food to give them. People lay on the ground for him. The food was too rich. Bars of chocolate. People cursed Mr. Goldman. People died because of the food. People died because they wanted it too much. And Dorff could come back and sit watching, and laugh and tell the German band to play "Rosamunda." Dorff would sit there sniffing in the sweet brown smoke from the chimneys, and laughing at Mr. Goldman, and calling him Cousin Arthur. It was a game. (*Pause.*) And sometimes he would speak in memory of Mr. Goldman's children. (*Pause.*) So when we were abandoned . . . at the end of the war . . . the Germans left us in a great hurry and someone led us to the German barracks outside the electric wire. On the tables were plates of frozen soup. The wine was yellow ice. There was frozen Schnapps. And we warmed and drank it all. Mr. Goldman was there. I remember him. We huddled together. They lit a fire from the benches, and sang. And Mr. Goldman told jokes. (*Long pause.*) But Dorff came back. He was shooting us all methodically, he would shoot in the nape of the neck, then throw the twisted body into the snow. We sat and waited for our turn. "Cousin," Dorff shouted, "Cousin Arthur, watch me for I shall never leave you." And then four boys, young boys on big horses, rode into the hut. They had fur hats. When he saw them, Dorff dropped his gun and fell on his knees. At first they did not fire at Dorff—the Russian boys. Then one of them got down from his great horse, and picked Dorff up, and carried Dorff out of the hut, and threw him onto the wire. Dorff screamed and pulled off the wire, and they threw him back onto it again. He stuck on the wire. And we all ran and tore at Dorff. We tore him to pieces. But I remember thinking: Mr. Goldman has stayed in the hut.

(*Silence.* MRS. ROSEN *enters the booth, undoes* GOLD-MAN's *tunic, looks at* GOLDMAN's *left armpit.* GOLD-MAN *is silent.* MRS. ROSEN *comes out of the booth.*)

MRS. ROSEN. Must have burned himself . . . no S.S. insignia there in the first place. Just burned a hole . . . the man just burned a hole in his armpit.

JUDGE. And his forearm—the Jewish number?

(MRS. ROSEN *looks at* GOLDMAN's *forearm.*)

MRS. ROSEN. Grafted over. The skin is grafted over. He must have grafted his number over. I was always looking for a lie. Once I told him that. I said to him, "Something about you makes me look for lies." But not this kind of lie, you understand.

JUDGE. You did not look hard enough, Mrs. Rosen.

MRS. ROSEN. (*Crosses back and sits.*) He sickened me

and that is why I must have lost my judgment. He will
have got to our agents. Bribed some of our agents. The
photographs were his photographs—the X-rays, his X-
rays.

(*Silence.*)

OLD WOMAN. I do not think we would have followed
where the Fuehrer led.

(GOLDMAN *raises his head, smiles at her.*)

JUDGE. What was the point of all this, Goldman?
MRS. ROSEN. He likes bad jokes.

(*Silence.*)

JUDGE. I understand his need to put a case. I understand a concern for Justice . . . a concern for law. I
understand his need to put a German in the dock—a German who would say what no German has said in the dock.
I understand that . . . (*The* JUDGE *pauses in thought.*)
I understand his guilt . . . even so, I would not have
done this—would never have done this.
MRS. ROSEN. He's more German than Jewish.

(*Silence.*)

JUDGE. Why did you do it? (*Silence.*) Haven't you done
us more harm than good? Is not what you have said
against us that will be remembered?

(*Silence.*)

MRS. ROSEN. He is an anti-semitic Jew.
JUDGE. (*Gently.*) Hasn't he the right?
MRS. ROSEN. (*Passionately.*) No, he has not the right.
(*She shouts.*) After all that has happened, nobody has the

right. (*Pause.*) He wanted to go to Calvary, Your Honor. So get out his nails. Take him, part his raiment. Cast your lots. This is the King of the Jews, Your Honor. Offer him vinegar. He wants to be crucified. Let him make his sacrifice. Your Honor, take the old sadist out and stone him. Take the old masochist out and scourge him.

JUDGE. Be quiet.

(GOLDMAN *laughs.*)

OLD WOMAN. Mr. Goldman, tell me. I was there.

(*Silence.* GOLDMAN *comes out of the booth and goes to the* OLD WOMAN *and embraces her.*)

GOLDMAN. (*Very gently to the* OLD WOMAN.) Sweetheart, you did me. Where's your brains? You're senile. You should never have spoke. Wanted to make some offering for them—something they'd understand. Wanted to let him take me up and swing me north, south, east and west. I wanted when the life was gone, they'd kiss my ass, kiss the turning cheeks of my swingin' ass, kiss my ass and call me sexy. Could I help my own dimensions? Could I help my sense of progress? Me? A messenger of peace. Best thing I ever did was break my glasses. Lost my contacts in a urinal. Should've stayed down there in the toilets.

JUDGE. Take him out. Gently. (*To* MRS. ROSEN.)

(*But* GOLDMAN *kicks at the* GUARDS. *He turns to the* OLD WOMAN *again.*)

GOLDMAN. (*Grinning.*) Was I bein' too hard on ya, sweetheart? (*He shouts.*) Sweetheart, if not *us* . . . who else? (*He wheels round to the audience. He looks at them.*) I chose ya because I knew ya. I chose ya because you're smart. I chose ya because you're Jewish. I chose ya because you're the chosen. I chose ya for remembrance. (GOLDMAN *begins to take off his shirt.*)

WOMAN. (*Desperately.*) You chose us because you love us.

GOLDMAN. (*Throwing out his arms to the audience.*) Battened down as we were, my brothers, my cousins, shunting from siding to siding, there was time. But after the wire I rode. I rode on Russian horses, on great black Russian horses. Every lamp post in Danzig a gallows. I clawed out their dead eyes with my nails. I rode on Russian horses and we battered Polish castles, we looted museums, we broke, we burned, we raped and we drank. We draped ourselves with golden tapestries, we covered our fingers with golden rings, we arrayed our horses with golden armor and we ate the German boys. We picked them up and ate them. We crushed them, we trampled them, we ravaged them in the snow—the snow that kept on falling. We kicked in their golden heads. We who were German and Jewish. We did that.

(*Pause.*)

JUDGE. You can leave the court. (*But now* GOLDMAN *goes to the glass booth. He takes the door key and locks himself inside. He takes off the rest of his clothes. The* GUARDS *beat on the door. The* JUDGE *descends from the bench and walks slowly to the naked* MAN *in the booth. But* GOLDMAN *is silent. Silence. Then the* OLD WOMAN *cries in anguish. Silence. Silence. Silence.*) Carry him out of the court.

(*The* GUARDS *gather round the booth examining it. The* COURT OFFICIALS *join them. For the moment they do not know how to get the man out. The LIGHTS fade.*)

CURTAIN

PROP LIST

OFF RIGHT:
Pocket comb—CHARLIE
Newspapers—CHARLIE
Brochure—CHARLIE
Date book—CHARLIE
Leather folder—CHARLIE
Tape recorder with mike—STEIGER and DURER
Cigar—CHARLIE
Lighter—CHARLIE
"25" cent piece—CHARLIE
Silver tray with coffeepot; cup and saucer—JACK
Silver tray with 3 beer glasses; 3 bottles of beer—JACK
Rembrandt painting—JACK and SAM
Poussin painting—JACK and SAM
Handbag—MRS. LEHMAN
In Safe:
Luger Pistol—GOLDMAN

ON STAGE:
House phone on wall U. S. of elevator
Fish food on fish tank
Cushion below urn
Flowers in vases L. and R. of urn
Raphael painting on easel

Desk:
T.V. set (folds into desk)
Ticker tape machine
2 ashtrays
1 cigarette box
1 telephone
1 lighter
1 wood humidor
1 cut glass decanter
1 brandy glass (pony)
C. drawer—box with pill
R. drawer—brown envelope with papers in it

Bar Top:
    7 assorted liquor bottles
    8 highball glasses
    Ice bucket with ice
    Ice tongs

Bar Bottom:
    6 liqueur bottles
    1 silver tray

Valet stand:
    Vest and coat
    Hand towel
    Bowl with lemon slices
    Watch and fob
    2 rings (1 wedding)

OFF LEFT:
    Roll of money and clip—GOLDMAN
    Doctor's bag with hypo and swab—KESSEL
    Brief case and papers—ROSEN
    Brief case with papers—GOLDMAN
    Pistol—STEIGER
    Pistol—DURER
    Pistol—ROSEN
    Box of flowers—FLOWER MAN
    TAPE—DURER
    Tape and suit on hanger—RUDIN
    Notebook and pencil—RUDIN
    2 rings and 1 watch with antique fob—GOLDMAN

In Booth:
    Glass of water
    2 microphones (1 on shelf—1 hanging D. L. corner)
    1 speaker (U. C. over door)
    List of witnesses and various papers in folder

On Judge's Bench:
    3 pitchers
    3 glasses
    3 sets of papers in folders
    1 gavel
    Pencils

On Prosecutor's Table:
Notebook and pencil
Papers

On Shelf Below Bench:
Notebook, pencil, papers—ROSEN
Notebook and pencil—STEIGER
Notebook and pencil—DURER

COSTUME PLOT

DR. KESSEL:
Gray glen plaid suit, striped shirt and bow tie, black shoes and socks

CHARLIE:

Act One—Scene 1:
Gray flannel suit, striped shirt and tie, black shoes and socks

Act One—Scene 2:
Blue dressing gown, slippers

Act Two—Scene 1:
Blue suit, white shirt, tie, black shoes and socks

STEIGER:

Act One:
Gray trousers and sweater, brown windbreaker, brown jodhpurs

Act Two:
Suntan trousers and shirt, brown sandals

Court:
Gray suit, white shirt, dark tie

ROSEN:

Act One:
Dark suit trimmed with leopard, leopard hat, dark shoes and stockings

Act Two:
Green smock, brown shoes

Court:
Brown smock, brown shoes and socks

GUARDS:
Israeli Army uniform

GOLDMAN:

Act One—Scene 1:
Brown suit, figured waistcoat, yellow shirt and red tie, brown shoes and socks

Act One—Scene 2:
Light brown suit, blue shirt and figured tie, brown shoes and socks, dark overcoat, dark hat

Act Two—Scene 1:
Suntan trousers and shirt, brown socks, old white sneakers

Act Two—Scene 2:
Nazi Colonel (SS) uniform, black boots, caps and black gloves

JUDGES:
Black judge's robes, white shirt and dark tie

MAROWSKI:
Rabbi costume with hat

MRS. LEVI:
Green suit and blouse, brown shoes

LANDAU:
Old trousers and shirt, old jacket

RUDIN:
Dark mohair suit, white shirt and figured tie, black shoes and socks

TZELNIKER:
Light tan suit, brown shoes and socks

JACK:
Black suit, white shirt and black tie

SAM:
Black suit, white shirt and black tie

MRS. LEHMAN:
Light summer dress, pocketbook and shoes

FLOWER MAN:
Dark trousers, green jacket with insignia, black shoes and socks

DURER:

Act One:
Brown trousers and shirt, brown car coat

Act Two:
Suntan trousers and shirt, brown sandals

Court:
Brown suit, brown shoes

PROSECUTOR:
Black robe, white shirt and black tie

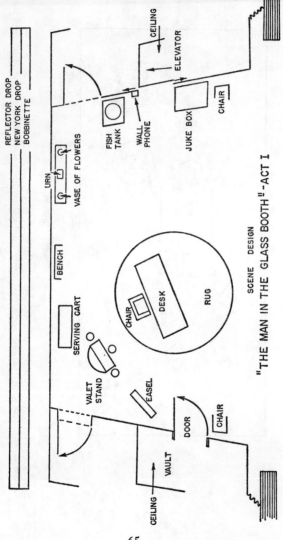

SCENE DESIGN

"THE MAN IN THE GLASS BOOTH"-ACT I

65

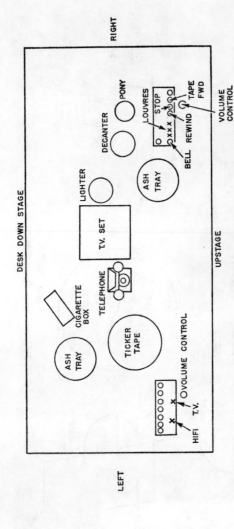

"DETAIL FOR DESK," ACT I

The desk top is marbelized and translucent. Twelve lumalines were used under the top and two fifty watt fresnels under the desk proper.

66

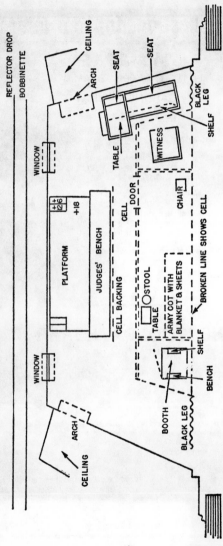

SCENE DESIGN.

"THE MAN IN THE GLASS BOOTH" – ACT II

Other Publications for Your Interest

SEA MARKS
(LITTLE THEATRE—DRAMA)

By GARDNER McKAY

1 woman, 1 man—Unit set

Winner of L.A. Drama Critics Circle Award "Best Play." This is the "funny, touching, bittersweet tale" (Sharbutt, A.P.) of a fisherman living on a remote island to the west of Ireland who has fallen in love with, in retrospect, a woman he's glimpsed only once. Unschooled in letter-writing, he tries his utmost to court by mail and, after a year-and-a-half, succeeds in arranging a rendezvous at which, to his surprise, she persuades him to live with her in Liverpool. Their love affair ends only when he is forced to return to the life he better understands. "A masterpiece." (The Tribune, Worcester, Mass.) "Utterly winning," (John Simon, New York Magazine.) "There's abundant humor, surprisingly honest humor, that grows between two impossible partners. The reaching out and the fearful withdrawal of two people who love each other but whose lives simply cannot be fused: a stubborn, decent, attractive and touching collision of temperments, honest in portraiture and direct in speech. High marks for SEA MARKS!" (Walter Kerr, New York Times.) "Fresh as a May morning. A lovely, tender and happily humorous love story." (Elliot Norton, Boston Herald American.) "It could easily last forever in actors' classrooms and audition studios." (Oliver, The New Yorker.)

(Royalty, $50–$35)

THE WOOLGATHERER
(LITTLE THEATRE—DRAMA)

By WILLIAM MASTROSIMONE

1 man, 1 woman—Interior

In a dreary Philadelphia apartment lives Rose, a shy and slightly creepy five-and-dime salesgirl. Into her life saunters Cliff, a hard-working, hard-drinking truck driver—who has picked up Rose and been invited back to her room. Rose is an innocent whose whole life centers around reveries and daydreams. He is rough and witty—but it's soon apparent—just as starved for love as she is. This little gem of a play was a recent success at New York's famed Circle Repertory starring Peter Weller and Patricia Wettig. Actors take note: The Woolgatherer has several excellent monologues. ". . . energy, compassion and theatrical sense are there."—N.Y. Times. ". . . another emotionally wrenching experience no theatre enthusiast should miss."—Rex Reed. "Mastrosimone writes consistently witty and sometimes lyrical dialogue."—New York Magazine. "(Mastrosimone) has a knack for composing wildly humorous lines at the same time that he is able to penetrate people's hearts and dreams."—Hollywood Reporter.

(Royalty, $50–$35)